Open Randomly

Fortune Cookies For the Soul

ALLY HAMILTON

DEDICATION

For Dylan and Devyn, my inspiration, my motivation, and
always, my best teachers.

CONTENTS

INTRODUCTION

I've been teaching yoga for many years, first in New York City where I was born and raised, and then in Los Angeles, where I moved in 2001, and currently reside. In 2009, I opened a yoga studio in Santa Monica called Yogis Anonymous with my then-husband and still-business partner (that's called advanced yoga, and you can read more about that journey in my upcoming book, "Yoga's Healing Power: Looking Inward for Change, Growth and Peace" due from Llewellyn Worldwide in July, 2016).

Demolition on the space we found began the same day I was in labor with our second baby, our daughter. Our son was two-and-a-half. To say it was a time of birthing would be to understate the situation. We didn't plan to do it all at once, that's just the way it happened.

When we opened the studio, we also created a Facebook page to let people know who and where we were. And at the same time, my husband was busily at work creating a website so we could stream video of our classes from our studio in California all over the globe. Before long, we had people on the fan page from everywhere.

I was doing my best to learn on-the-job. It was my first foray into the world of social media, and I understood you only had three seconds to grab and keep someone's attention, so I posted quotes that I found inspirational, and lots of posters of animals photoshopped in yoga poses, because apparently, people dig that.

But my husband was encouraging me to use the page to speak to people from my heart, the way I try to do when I teach. And I couldn't figure out how to do that in three seconds, so one day I posted an essay about loss. I did an English major and a Psychology minor at Columbia University, but it had been years since I'd written anything that anyone else was going to read. When I hit "post", my heart was racing and my hands were shaking, because we had about 30,000 people on the page at that point, and I felt vulnerable and exposed. I figured my mom, and maybe four other people would "like" it, and I'd go back to animal posters, but it took off in a way I could not have imagined.

It seemed people wanted to connect in a real, raw way, and a conversation emerged on the page that was exciting and honest and enthusiastic. So, a few days later, I did it again, and the same thing happened. And thus, the blog was also born.

As I write this, there are almost 200,000 people on the page, and it's growing all the time. This still amazes me. I never thought a virtual world could provide a deep, meaningful place for connection to happen, but it did, and it continues to do so. I've exchanged private messages and emails with people from all over the world, none of whom I would have crossed paths with any other way. I've done life-coaching sessions over Skype from my living room to the South of France, Baltimore, and Burbank. And often, someone shows up in person at the studio, and tells me they read the blog, and we hug like old friends.

For quite some time, there have been a chorus of people asking for a book. About two years ago, a student approached me (the amazing Dana Newman) and said she was a literary agent and asked if I had representation. She told me I should write a book proposal. It took me about nine months and nine million revisions (and incredible patience on her part), but I did it, and she sold it. Writing that book was one of the most challenging labors of love I've ever been through, but I was also gifted with an incredible editor (Angela Wix), and a few good friends who are published, well-respected writers (Dani Shapiro, who wrote the most amazing foreword for the book, Mark Sarvas, who was there to talk me off the ledge on more than a few occasions, and generally advise me whenever I felt overwhelmed, and Claire Bidwell Smith, who relates to the life of a writer with young kids, and is always ready to let the kids go nuts while we sit together laughing at the dining room table).

I could not be happier with the way the book came out, and I can't wait for you to read it, but as I write this, we have almost a year until publication day. And in the meantime, many of you amazing blog readers have been asking for a compilation of the blog posts. I get that. It's nice to have something physical you can hold and open. I was thinking about that a few weeks ago, after I turned in the final draft of my book and wondered what to do over the next year (because, you know, running after two small children, and co-running two businesses while maintaining a full teaching schedule just isn't enough!) And I was talking to my partner/ex about the idea of a compilation book, and the title "Open Randomly" popped into my head. I thought it would be useful to group the posts together under certain themes, but that a person could just open to any page on any given day, and see what the topic was. Kind of like a fortune cookie for your soul.

So here we are. I've picked 60 of the most popular blog posts and edited them, and I hope they will be exactly what you need whenever you open this little book that represents such a big part of my heart and my gratitude for the blog, and all the beauty that's grown from it. I think of this book as the, "we're all in it together" part; when I look at the posts from a distance, I see that they're really dealing with the universal issues we all face as we move through this experience of being human. The next book is the "what to do about it" part, where I dive into the yogic philosophy behind the modern-world stories, and offer tangible tools for healing to make real shifts in your life if you're feeling called to do that. I also offer many examples from my own life and history, mistakes I made along the way, and where I've ended up today. I hope you'll enjoy this little book, and I can't wait to put the next one in your hands. If only I knew how to speed up time in that regard! Thank you for your support, your enthusiasm, and your open hearts.

Sending you love, as I always am,

Ally Hamilton

CHAPTER 1: THE RELATIONSHIP YOU'RE HAVING WITH YOURSELF

The relationship you're having with yourself is the foundation for all the relationships you're having in your life. If you aren't coming from a place of love, love is not going to magically blossom around you. All the posts in this section have to do with what is at your core, and will hopefully encourage you to do the work to learn to love yourself.

You Don't Have to Have Braids

Last week, I took my daughter with me when I went to get my toenails painted, and they always do her nails, too. It's a little ritual once in awhile, while her brother is in school, and I pick her up earlier from Kindergarten. As I was paying for my pedicure, I noticed that the woman who'd painted my daughter's nails was now finishing a second braid in her hair. I went and stood next to her, and when she was done, we thanked her, and we left. We weren't three feet out of the salon when my daughter looked up at me and said, "I didn't want braids." When I asked her why she didn't just say that, she kind of shrugged her shoulders at me.

My daughter is a firecracker at home. She has no problem telling any of us what she wants or does not want, in a strong, assertive way. Just ask her brother. But when she doesn't know people, she can be shy and quiet. She's also sensitive and caring. She's a watcher. She asked me if she could take the braids out, and of course I said she could.

When we got in the car, I told her it was really important that she understand that she gets to decide what happens to her own hair. Her own body. Her own nails. And that it's okay to say, "No thank you, I don't want braids." I asked her to say it to me a few times, for practice. I asked her to say it a little more loudly each time. By the third or fourth time, she was yelling it out the window, laughing, and I was yelling it with her, "I don't want braids!!" It's so simple, right? But it's not always so easy to say what we want, or do not want, or to ask for what we need. I will not stop working with my daughter on this, because it's a big part of our self-esteem, feeling that we should value our feelings and act on our own behalf.

Sometimes we take care of other people at our own expense. We feel something inside, but we keep it inside because we don't want to hurt someone's feelings, or we tell ourselves it isn't that big of a deal. If you make a habit out of that, you're making a habit out of putting other people's needs and wants ahead of your own. When we make sacrifices for those we love because it feels good, that's one thing. But when we make it a way of life to always put other people's feelings ahead of ours, we're in trouble. It won't be long before we can't even identify what we're feeling, let alone act on it.

There's a difference between generosity, and care-taking or people pleasing. If you grew up feeling you needed to earn love, this easily may have followed you into your adult life. You may fear speaking up, or standing up for yourself, because you think if you do, love may be withdrawn, or people might not like you. Maybe it's such an ingrained way of being, you don't even realize you're doing it. Do you say, "Sorry!" when someone bumps into you? I'm laughing, because I do that sometimes, and then, two seconds later, I'm like, "Why am I apologizing?" Am I saying, "I'm sorry you aren't paying attention"? Or am I saying, "I'm sorry I'm taking up space"? That's a pretty important distinction, right?

You don't have to apologize for your feelings. You may not get everything you want or need, but it never hurts to ask. At least that way, you've communicated clearly, and that makes everything simpler. If a person doesn't care about how you feel, you can then decide whether it's a relationship you want to pursue, or one to which you want to be devoting time and energy, or not so much. If you speak up and a person cannot give you what you need or want, at least you both understand that. You aren't left in the murky waters of wondering whether you've been mis-understood or disrespected or unseen.

Being accountable for how we feel and what's happen-ing within us is a gift we give ourselves, and everyone we encounter. There are enough mysteries in life. Even if you're clear about how you feel in every given moment, you're still going to be part of the mystery that's happening around us, and you're still going to surprise yourself by the things you sometimes want or think or dwell upon. Know-ing yourself takes work and time, and so does knowing other people. Don't ever be sorry for taking up space, and don't ever get braids if you don't want them. Say it with me if you need to, "I don't want braids!!"

Starve Your Inner Critic

If you're suffering from self-loathing and a loud inner critic, you're in the worst kind of prison. You can't evict your inner voice, so if it's harsh, shaming and unforgiving, there's nowhere to run. If you'd categorize the way you're speaking to yourself as abusive, were you to hear the same words coming from someone else's mouth, then it's time to stage a take-down, because that's no way to live.

Sometimes we absorb the way we were spoken to as we were growing up. Not everyone is received with love; not everyone is nurtured. Author and inspirational speaker Peggy O'Mara has a quote, "The way we talk to our children becomes their inner voice." I think there's a lot of truth to that, but it isn't always the whole story. You may have come from an incredibly loving family, but suffered unkindness at school. Scared and confused children can be mean, as can those who feel powerless at home. Events may have occurred that made you doubt yourself, or question your ideas about your own worth. Sometimes we're going along just fine, and then we're completely derailed by a romantic relationship, or an interaction with someone who has power over us, and it's a game-changer. Other times, we learn and we grow and we look back and feel intense shame for certain choices we made, or ways we let ourselves or others down.

There are all kinds of reasons that voice in our heads can become critical and unrelenting. Coming out of abuse is another one. Feeling like love can be withdrawn at any time will also do it, because any time you fail to meet your own unrealistic expectations of perfection, you've set yourself up for the punishing sting of pain and disappointment. There are many ways we can betray our own tender hearts.

The thing is, in order to shine and to share, you have to have some belief in yourself. And to be straight with you, not believing in yourself is the worst kind of hubris. It's not a level playing field, but we've all been given the gift of a body, some time here on earth, and the ability to love deeply. Squandering those gifts is the equivalent of hijacking your experience here. You can look back and rant and rave and point fingers. You can write a dissertation about why you are the way you are, and why it isn't your fault, but time will keep on ticking, and you can't have it back.

We all make mistakes. We've all suffered loss to some degree or another, along with heartache, grief, regret, fear, confusion, shame, doubt and longing. If we're lucky, we've also tasted joy and gratitude, love, kindness and connection. It's a mixed bag here on planet earth, but it's definitely an interesting ride. Getting bogged down in rage is no way to travel. There are so many tools available, so many paths of liberation, so many ways to enjoy the gifts we've been given. You really don't want to rob yourself of all the beauty available here.

How do you starve an inner critic and feed a loving voice? I'm sure there are many tools, but the ones I've tested personally are the physical yoga practice, and seated meditation. There's a saying, "How you do anything is how you do everything", and I believe that to be the truth. If you're critical of yourself out in the world, the same will hold true when you're on your yoga mat. But if you stick with it and make it about breathing deeply and consciously, and not about how you look or what's happening around you, a miraculous thing will happen. You'll start to take the road marked "Inward", so you can take a look around and start dealing with anything that isn't serving you. You can start to observe yourself from the inside out, and build the muscle called compassion. You can work on the quality of patience. You can calm your nervous system with your breath. You can create enough space between your thoughts to get a taste of something called peace. And you can develop the ability to witness your tendencies, your thoughts and your feelings. You can start to recognize that you don't have to believe everything you think, as the saying goes. You can start to choose better thoughts. Over time, you can feed a loving voice so it grows and strengthens and takes over your life. It just takes work and determination. I'm always waiting for you online if you need help!

The Dangers of Low Self-Esteem

When I was in college, I used to babysit for this family. They had the most adorable little girl, and I loved her. Over the summer, I was with her every day. During the school year, I'd babysit some nights and weekends. She was a little sweetheart, but the mom and dad were not so wonderful. First of all, they didn't pay me a competitive hourly rate. And then they'd always "round down", so if they were fifteen minutes past the hour, they just wouldn't count that. To be fair, I wasn't assertive at that time in my life, I wasn't used to standing up for myself. So I'd rev myself up to talk to them once in awhile about a higher rate, but they'd always say they couldn't afford it. And I was attached to their daughter, and she was attached to me, too, so I'd stay. Often, they'd also come home a lot later than we'd agreed they would. Basically, it was an opportunity for me to practice self-respect and to set boundaries, but I just wasn't there yet.

That wasn't the only time I experienced this kind of

thing. I worked for a woman who made jewelry, and helped her at trade shows. Sometimes she'd be really nice, and other times she'd be awful. Not surprisingly, I met her through the family I just mentioned. I only worked for this woman for a few months, but that was enough. I never knew what to expect. Some days I'd go in and she'd be lovely, and full of compliments, and other days I'd go in and she would be rude and nasty. I think I was about seventeen at the time, and I just didn't know how to handle it. "I quit" was a tough one for me then. Eventually, I did quit because it was just such a miserable scene.

I've had lots of experiences with people over the years when I didn't stand up for myself and should have. There was another woman with a baby I worked with over one summer. She was a new mom, and a nervous one. She'd asked me to stay with her son while she went back to work part-time, but that never happened. Instead, I'd go over and she would stay, too, and I'd end up changing diapers and making bottles and playing with the baby, getting lunch for the mom, or throwing in a load of laundry. Sometimes I'd prep dinner. I didn't mind, because most of the time she was fun to hang out with, but when her girlfriends came over she treated me like crap. She'd be rude and bossy and disrespectful, like a mean girl in high school. Once, she made fun of me while I was getting drinks for her and her friends. Something about my needing a haircut or something, and all these women laughed in the other room, and I blinked back tears in the kitchen.

Years later, I taught at a yoga studio owned by a guy who was also unpredictable. Sometimes awesome, sometimes mean. I quit after a few months because by then, I had the tools to get myself out of situations that were insulting and painful to my heart. The only reason we allow other people to devalue us or treat us poorly is if some part of us believes we aren't worthy of more. Low self-esteem is not only painful, it's dangerous. And it often goes hand-in-hand with people-pleasing tendencies. If we doubt our worth, we look outward for reassurance and approval. And at that point, it's a crap shoot. Maybe you'll get lucky, and only encounter kind, stable, ethical people, but I highly doubt it. You might interact with people who have personality disorders that render them incapable of empathy or consistency. You might run into people who are controlling or manipulative because they've hardened themselves. There are many ways you can get yourself into trouble when you don't recognize what a miracle you are. And I mean that sincerely. I don't say it to make you blush, I say it to give you a prod in the ass if you need one. Because it's my opinion that we're all here to shine, to uncover whatever gifts we've been given, and to share them freely. You can't do that, and doubt your worth, simultaneously.

How is it possible we have seven billion people on the planet, but only one of you? Those are pretty amazing odds, and the only safe bet is that you have something to give that only you can. If you're bogged down in rage or shame or blame, if you're numbing yourself out or running or denying your pain, it's really time to stop doing that.

The time is always now. If you're allowing yourself to be mistreated, get help today. Find a great therapist. Ask for support. You can't allow yourself to be bruised and battered for too long, and expect life to feel good. If you doubt your worth, figure out why that is, and when that started. Because nothing else is going to fall into place until you do. The relationship you're having with yourself is the groundwork for all the relationships in your life. You are not here to let other people walk on you, or treat you badly. You are not here to teach people the right and kind way to behave, unless you have children. It is not your job to wait for someone to see the light, nor can you show it to another person. You can love people who don't know how to love, but it hurts like hell. You can recognize that someone may be treating you poorly because they don't know how to do anything else. You can feel empathy for someone's painful or abusive history, or for their struggle with mental illness or depression. but you cannot allow yourself to be treated without decency or respect.

You are as worthy of love as anyone else walking the planet. My personal belief is that we're made of energy, and that energy is love. I think we come into this world and sometimes we forget who we are. Sometimes we're hurt or disappointed and we harden ourselves to get by. You might have to do your childhood that way depending on the circumstances, but you don't have to do your whole life like that. That would be such a waste, and such a tragedy. Tools exist. Shifts are possible. You can feel good about yourself, you can learn to stand up for yourself the way you would for anyone else you love. But you might have some serious healing to do before you get there, and I'd really suggest you get on that. Healing takes work, but it's doable. You just have to start.

Grappling with Your Truth

Most of us know what's true for us long before we act on it, especially when we're talking about making huge life shifts. Sometimes we agonize for weeks, months, or even years, because so much hinges on maintaining the status quo. This can happen in our personal and professional lives. People stay in jobs that crush their souls for all kinds of reasons. Some are practical—they need to keep a roof over their heads and food in their refrigerators. Or they need health insurance for themselves and their families. Sometimes the reasons have more to do with low self-esteem, or a lack of self-respect. People tell themselves every day that they are not good enough, that they don't measure up, that they should be thankful for what they have, because who are they to think that things could be different? Who are they to pursue their dreams? There are many reasons we might convince ourselves we're stuck. And when you're speaking about the necessities of life, of course those are real. But if you're in a job that's sucking the life out of you, I wouldn't accept that as "the way things have to be." I'd do everything in your power to seek out another opportunity somewhere, because 80 hours a week is a lot of time to spend feeling like you want to scream.

And of course it happens in relationships, too. Sometimes two people come together, and despite all their best efforts, they grow in different directions. Maybe they met when they both had healing to do, and attempted to cover their individual pain with a relationship. Maybe there are kids in the mix, and now it's brutal. Staying is painful, and leaving is painful. Sometimes the choice is figuring out the least painful option. It's human to agonize when we're faced with a decision that impacts the people we love. But ultimately, if you're in a situation that's crushing you, you'll never be able to nurture yourself, or anyone else to the best of your ability. Maybe you can get creative. Maybe you can go for radical honesty with your partner, and come up with a way to stay, and not feel like you're losing yourself, and maybe you can't. But allowing your light to go out is never the way. Numbing yourself or editing yourself until there's almost nothing left of you won't serve anyone. Distracting yourself, running, denying, keeping everything on the surface level will not be sustainable for the long haul.

So what do you do? I think first you get quiet so you can really allow yourself to feel whatever it is you're feeling. And face those realities head on. There's no point hiding from yourself. That doesn't mean you have to act on your feelings. It's just that it's such a relief to acknowledge them, to lean into them, to accept them, and accept yourself. Then, at least, you're dealing with your own truth. Getting support from someone objective is also a great idea. And communicating honestly is a must.

I don't believe anyone would thank you for keeping them in the dark, or staying in something out of guilt, shame or pity. Maybe you can resurrect the thing. But the only chance you have, is if you start building with blocks of truth. You can't build anything that lasts on top of lies, bitterness, resentment or rage. You want to be seen, right? You want someone to see you, to understand you, to cherish you for the person you are. But you give no one the opportunity to do that if you repress what's real for you. Is it scary to start a conversation that may change the course of your life, and the lives of those you love? Absolutely. But it's less scary than decades of betrayals, emotional or otherwise. And I'm talking about the betrayal of your own heart, as much as anything else, here. If you want to be at peace, you have to allow what is true for you to rise to the surface and spill out of your mouth, kindly, confidently, and with compassion.

Boundaries

Being kind and understanding is very different than allowing yourself to be abused, mistreated or disrespected. Sometimes there's a thin line between compassion for other people, and abuse of self. Being spiritual does not mean we allow ourselves to be injured, dumped on, taken advantage of, or treated like a doormat. When you've lost your self-respect and you've allowed your tender heart to be handled in a reckless way, you've betrayed the most vulnerable part of yourself, and that's the source of your light and your strength. There is no true spiritual practice that demands you hand that over.

Sometimes I get emails from people wondering where the line is. I'll tell you what I think. I think in order to help, nurture or support anyone else, we have to be doing those things for ourselves, first. You can't be a source of strength for anyone if you're doubting your worth. And if someone is treating you badly, your job is to remove yourself from that situation. It doesn't necessarily mean you have to cut this person out of your life (although it will mean that in some instances), but before you can figure out what to do or how to respond, you have to get yourself to a safe space. I mean that physically, mentally and emotionally. You are not here to participate in the dimming of your light, or the crushing of your spirit.

We can recognize when people we love are in pain, and of course it's natural to want to help. But we can't save other people, or fix them, or make them see how beautiful they are. And when a person is in acute pain, you're likely to get some spillover.

This is where boundaries come into play. Standing up for yourself does not run counter to having empathy. You empathize, but you get the hell out of Dodge and do that from a distance where you can still honor and protect yourself. If someone is in a space where they abuse you, neglect you, belittle you, or discard you like trash, you really can't participate in that and feel good about yourself. It's okay, and it's imperative, to say no sometimes. "No, this is not okay for me." Say it out loud if you need to, practice speaking the words. You deserve love and kindness and respect as much as anyone else, and you serve no one by forgetting that, or compromising your own sense of what's right.

Sometimes we find ourselves in situations we never thought we'd allow. I think most of us have been there at least once. Sometimes it's romantic relationships, sometimes it's familial, once in awhile we allow ourselves to be abused by a "friend" or co-worker or boss. Maybe it's insidious. Things start out well enough, but little by little they deteriorate, until one day we wake up and wonder what happened, and how exactly we landed ourselves in this painful situation.

Start where you are. If you're being abused in any way, get yourself some help. Gather yourself up and remember your work here is to love and to shine and to connect. And do whatever you need to do to make yourself safe. That's your baseline job. That's the number one thing. Because until that basic need is met, until it's safe for you to be vulnerable, you won't be living.

I Think I Can, I Think I Can

Do you remember the story about "The Little Engine That Could"? In retrospect I think it's brilliant. You will be alone with your thoughts for most of your life. The quality of your internal dialogue will be the greatest influence on the experience you have as you move through your days. You know the Henry Ford quote? "Whether you think you can, or whether you think you can't, you're right." And I mention that with the full understanding that the playing field is not level, that some people will come into this world with advantages, and some people will have to fight for every single break they get. Nonetheless, a person's way of thinking has a huge impact upon the way life will feel, regardless of advantages and obstacles.

If you are full of fear and doubt and negativity and judgment, you are probably not going to experience a lot of joy. Because you're going to walk through the world in a defensive manner, in a hopeless manner, in an angry and resentful way. If you fill your caboose with stories about every way you've been hurt and disappointed, you're just not going to make it up that hill, because that stuff is heavy.

We are energetic beings. Wherever we go, we spread energy, and we take it in, as well. If you're feeling down and dark and depressed, it will affect the way you carry yourself, and the energy you're spreading as you go about your day. If you are in a frame of mind that says, "Everyone is out to get me", or, "I never get any breaks", or "People suck", believe me, it will be something people can feel. They may not know exactly what they're feeling, but chances are, they're going to move away from you, not toward you, thus strengthening your idea that people suck. I'm not talking about tough times here, so please don't misunderstand me. If something heartbreaking happens, you have to feel your feelings around all of that, and take your time. What I'm talking about is a way of being, your general outlook. And of course this is going to be shaped by your history, but at a certain point, we all have to take the reins.

On the other hand, if you're on a track that says, "You know, things aren't perfect but I have my health. I have a place to call home. I have food in my refrigerator. I have people in my life who love me, and people I love with my whole heart. There are damaged people in the world, but there are also so many good people. And life can be devastating, but it can also be devastatingly beautiful. I'm going to do whatever I can with whatever I've got to try to make this world a little brighter", I guarantee you that will also affect the way you move through your day. The more you can pick your mind up and bring it back to all the amazing things you do have, the more thankful you will feel. And the more you focus on all the things you don't have yet, that aren't going well, that haven't unfolded the way you'd like, that other people have and you don't, the more miserable you will be.

Yes, life will bring circumstances, and some of them will break your heart wide open. You can let those experiences close you and harden you. You can decide life is something to get through. You can say things like, "I'm killing time." Or you can let those experiences open you and soften you. You can keep picking the mind up and bringing it back to love. I'm not saying everything in your life will be magically perfect if you do that. I'm saying that being in a state of gratitude and coming from abundance feels so much better than being angry and shut down.

And being kind to yourself is a huge part of the equation, because if your inner voice is harsh, unforgiving and merciless, wow are you going to suffer. You can beat yourself down into a state of loneliness and confusion and shame if you're not careful. You can come to believe you are totally alone and no one cares. That's a lie, of course, but you can convince yourself it's true if the mind is dark enough, and you can wear your despair and disappointment on your sleeve.

Alternatively, you can work on feeding a loving voice, a kind, compassionate, caring voice. Because whatever you feed will grow and strengthen. Feed love. Feed it with everything you've got. Be vigilant about it. Because what you think absolutely affects how you feel, and how you feel influences what you say and do, the level of compassion you extend to yourself and others, your ability to forgive your own mistakes and those of all the other humans around you, your likelihood of finding your purpose, of moving in the direction of that inner, burning Yes… all these things require love. If all that sounds good to you, you've got to put your train on the Love track. And don't just think you can, know you can. I know you can.

Don't Wait

Waiting can be a particular kind of agony, whether we're waiting for a call, an email response, the results of a test, a job interview, or a first date. But we never know what's going to happen, even though we like to think we do. Tomorrow isn't promised, and we can make all the plans we like, we can create our routines and try to make order out of chaos, but there's no getting around that truth. And for many people there's the impulse to run from it, but I think if you accept and embrace that you don't know what's coming, or how much time you've got, it can also inspire you. A little fire under your ass can be a great thing. That way you don't get caught up in the idea that you can "waste" time, or "kill" time, because you know it's precious.

Why do we agonize when we're waiting for the phone to ring? Do we really think our happiness lies in the outcome? People will like us and dig us and understand us, and other people will not do any of those things. The news will be good, there won't be any news, or the news will be bad. The real issue isn't the news. It's how you're spending your time and energy. Waiting is probably not a great use of your time, because it takes you out of the power seat, and I don't mean power over other people, I mean the power you can exert over how you're going to use the time you have. If you have a dream, if you have something to say, something to offer, you just keep going. There's no need to wait. If you keep directing your energy toward spreading some love with every day you've got, I really believe that momentum will build on itself. Giving for the sake of giving is the reward. It happens as you're doing it. If you're giving to get, that's another thing altogether.

Is it okay to want good things in your life? Love, companionship, affection, at least one person who sees you and knows you and cherishes you? Of course. But if a person isn't running in your direction, and I mean this whether we're talking about a romantic or a professional interest, keep going. They can catch up if it's the right thing. Waiting feels like sh&t. Waiting for someone's approval, acknowledgement, love, attention, respect? Screw that. If a person doesn't have it to give, get going. Give it to yourself, and keep giving it to yourself, and don't let anyone or anything cause you to doubt your ability to offer something only you can. There's only one of you, in a world of billions. You think you were put here to wait? I don't.

And to be clear, I'm not talking about patience, which is something else. We all need patience in this world. Sometimes we have to be patient with ourselves, and our inclination to give someone else power over us. Maybe we have healing to do. Maybe we doubt whether we're lovable at our very core. Maybe we have to be patient with someone we love. I'm not talking about that.

I'm talking about hours, afternoons, days, weeks when most of your energy is spent waiting for something to happen, instead of living each beautiful day you're given in awe and wonder and gratitude, or in deep sadness if that's where it's at. But you don't want to allow your energy, your essence to be derailed while you obsess over what someone else might or might not do, how someone else might or might not reward you, how you might or might not be received and understood, what calamity might or might not befall you. That's what I'm talking about.

At a certain point, you have to take action. You can't wait for some magical time in the future when life is going to feel good, you have to take action to move it in that direction yourself.

Bearing an Untold Story

Last night I had a nightmare. I don't have them often, but when I do, they're always variations on a theme. I'm in serious danger, or someone I love is in danger, and I'm trying to yell for help, but no sound comes out. I open my mouth, but where I want the scream to happen, there's only a whisper and I realize I won't make it. No one will come. Eventually, I wake up with the effort of trying to scream.

When I was twenty-six I had surgery to remove what turned out to be a benign tumor. I was under general anesthesia and at some point during the surgery, I woke up on the table. Apparently, this is not uncommon. My arms and legs were strapped down and it was freezing in the room. It's the coldest I've ever felt. I could hear music playing, and my doctor in conversation with someone assisting her. I could feel incredible pressure in my chest, and a pulling sensation that was horrible. I was terrified. I tried to say, "I'm awake, I can feel what's happening." But I couldn't find the words, I couldn't locate the language. I guess eventually I was able to groan, because they gave me more anesthesia, and I went under again.

Having nightmares once in awhile is not a terrible thing. But I share this story with you because some people live this way. They have some deep truth that's screaming to get out, but they can't find the words to express it. They can't locate the language. Too many people live in silent agony, thinking their feelings don't really matter. Or their family and friends wouldn't understand. Or whatever their truth is, it's impractical, and something to hide. You get one life in the body you're in, that much we know. You get one life with the parents you have, with the siblings you do or don't have, with the children you have or you don't. One life with these particular experiences and memories and thoughts and feelings. If you have a truth burning to get out, you push it down at your own peril. And you deny those in your one, beautiful life, the opportunity to know you and see you and celebrate you.

If you learned along the way that your feelings are not important, that you don't matter or are invisible, you really need to unlearn that. You're here to love and to shine and to be you. No one else can do that. You might need some help if you have a history of pushing things down, or if your pattern is to explode from time to time--if the truth comes out, but it comes out bent and ragged from the pressure of having been denied, if it comes out loud and hard and cold, and not at all as you'd meant it to. The thing is, you know the language of your calm truth; it's inside you. You just might not have accessed it yet. It's your intuition, and it has a quiet, beautiful voice. There are so many healing modalities that are designed to help us tune into it. Yoga worked for me, which is why I teach. Figuring out what works for you is the most important work you'll do, because if you can't access the language to express your deepest truths, you'll never be happy, and the world will be robbed of a song only you can sing.

You Can't Run

Recently I was traveling, and happened to sit next to a man on a long flight. As these things go, we struck up a conversation that was interrupted several times by one or the other of my kids, but over the course of the flight, I pretty much heard his life story. When he found out I was a yoga teacher, he perked up, and began asking me questions about his legs. He's a serious runner, swimmer and cyclist, and has been for his whole life. He does triathlons and marathons and 5k's and he's done Ironman several times. But over the last year, his legs started giving out. He'd be running a few miles, or swimming a short distance, or cycling around his neighborhood trails, and suddenly his legs would lose their steam, cramp up, refuse to go on.

He's been to all kinds of doctors, he's had MRIs, been to PT, you name it, and no one can find anything physically wrong. So I asked him if anything had happened in the last year, anything emotional. And he looked at me like I was a little crazy, and then admitted he'd been through a painful divorce, and lost his mother, all in the same year. I asked him if running, cycling and swimming were coping mechanisms for him. Obviously, they're healthy activities, but like anything else, when done to the extreme, they can be debilitating. And he said without a doubt, these were the resources he used to "get through his childhood and teenage years."

It turns out he comes from an abusive and alcoholic family, and he grew up feeling unsafe, unseen and unheard. But he found relief by joining the swim team, the track team, and cycling to and from school when he got old enough. He said those were the times he could forget his life, the awful stuff that was happening at home, the rage he felt toward his dad, and the powerlessness he felt regarding his mom, whom he adored but couldn't save. He said he'd been struggling with depression for most of his life, but it had taken a turn over the last year, and that he'd sought help from a therapist. He went on antidepressants for several months, but then stopped them cold turkey, thinking they might be the reason his legs were giving out. He said he'd never really wanted to be on meds in the first place, but also that they had helped.

Anyway, he's been off his medication for months, and still the legs won't do what he wants them to do. He said there have been moments when he's so frustrated on a run, or a ride, that if he had a knife with him, he would have stabbed himself in the quadriceps. That's grief and rage and pain for you. And I'm sharing this with you, with his permission, because I don't think it's all that uncommon.

The body is with us through everything. We're energetic creatures, and we both absorb and emit energy. If you grew up in a war zone, you're probably familiar with cowering, crouching, covering your head and face with your arms, making yourself invisible or invaluable. Children who grow up this way don't spend time discovering who they are or what makes them happy. They're too focused on survival and how to maneuver or help or be "good enough" to stop the abuse, to consider things like what makes them happy, or what they'd like to be doing on any particular afternoon. When you worry for your own safety, or your mother's, when you feel terrified and helpless, believe me, this stuff gets stored in your body. Maybe you grind your teeth or you have migraines, or you walk around with your shoulders up around your ears all the time, or you have ulcers, or you're loathe to leave the safe space of your house (if you've managed to create a safe space for yourself). Trauma lives in the body, and unless you give it an outlet, unless you acknowledge its existence, you will carry it with you.

We all have our coping mechanisms, and some of them are healthy, and some of them are not. Even exercise, widely accepted as a healthy outlet, can become a source of addiction for people. In this particular case, we have a man running, swimming, cycling away from a lifetime of pain. And you know, you just can't outrun this stuff. At a certain point, if you don't stop, and get still, and allow the pain to wash over you, it will own you for your entire life. I think his legs are giving out because his heart is in need of his kind attention. And I think he knows that, because he sought help from a therapist. But it was still hard for him to accept that the source of his frustration with his legs could be emotional. Of course I can't know this for sure. But there's nothing physically wrong. And my guess is that once he allows himself to really examine and lean into all that grief and rage and guilt and shame (although he's blameless), it will lose its grip on him. I think his body is giving out so that he has no option but to try things another way, because being on the run isn't working anymore.

And for most of us, this is what it takes. Most people will not wake up one day and decide to face their pain, most people will have to be pushed to do that. Pushed into acknowledging that what they've been doing simply isn't working. Life has to become unmanageable and unlivable before the large majority of people will opt to work with their grief. I think this is because we fear the pain will overwhelm us, when the reality is, not facing it is what does that. Yes, he'll probably be deeply uncomfortable, or enraged or heartbroken for the short-term. He has a lot to process. The loss of his childhood, for one. The loss of his innocence. Some things are taken from us that we can never have back, and some mourning is in order for loss like that. The loss of his mother, for example. The loss of his marriage, his house, many of his friends, his routine, his place in the world. But this is what's in his path. You can't cycle over that stuff. You can't swim underneath it. You can't run away from it. You have to turn around, sit down, and open to it. Then you can release the heat of it, the rage of it, the burning grief of it. And then, my guess is, you can get back on your feet and find your legs are working again, and that they'll take you where you want to go, instead of where you need to go. That makes all the difference in the world, and that isn't something that's going to show up in an MRI. This stuff I'm talking about is the business of your heart, your mind, and your emotional body. And if you want to be at peace, you're going to have to get acquainted with all three.

CHAPTER 2: RELATIONSHIPS YOU'RE HAVING WITH OTHERS

Some of the best stuff in life comes through connection. We come into this world needing to be held, comforted, fed and nurtured. As we grow, coming from a foundation of love and security enables us to venture out into the world with confidence. Shared experience is so reassuring. Even a genuine smile, shared with a stranger, reminds us that we are not alone.

Sometimes we don't grow out of love, though. Sometimes we're born into pain and confusion, and other people and the world at large become frightening and unpredictable. Sometimes we're taught that we have to earn love and worthiness, or that our value lies in what we can do for other people. Life is not easy if we aren't able to connect, to feel a part of the flow, to know we have a few people who truly see, understand and cherish us. There's no doubt we have to cultivate a loving inner environment in order to spread and create love around us, but sometimes our relationships are plagued with ancient history and fear. Learning to open and trust is a process, but it's one you want to move through, so you don't miss out on some of the best stuff in life.

The Part That is Personal

Often I get emails from people who tell me their relationships would be wonderful, if only their partner would change. And sometimes they tell me they've been to therapy hoping that would help, but there hasn't been any movement. Here's the thing. We can never change other people. No one can ever change us, either, unless we want to make a shift. And you can find yourself at a real stalemate, and start to feel hopeless and stuck.

But just as we can never change other people, we are also not set in stone. You can always change what you are doing, and there's so much power in that. When you look at the situations in your life, the story to pay attention to is not the one about what this person did, or how things unfolded in ways you couldn't have imagined, or how something beautiful turned into something painful. I mean, you can examine all of that, but the thing you really want to dive into, is the story of your own participation.

Sometimes people get very clear on the "not taking things personally" part, and that's wonderful. If someone is abusive, cruel, unkind, dismissive, thoughtless or disrespectful, that's a reflection of where they are on their particular journey at this point in time; it is not a reflection of anything lacking within you. But, and this is an important "but", what is about you is your decision to continue to interact with people who don't know how to do anything but hurt you. That part is the personal part, that's the part you want to understand.

We're not always talking about awful, abusive situations. Sometimes it's just a matter of the spark going out. People take their partners or loved ones for granted all the time. Sometimes we think we have people all figured out, and we don't have to pay attention anymore, but everyone and everything is in a constant state of flux. You are not the you of five years ago, and neither is anyone else. You can't ever peg anyone, but you can stop looking and listening and appreciating and cherishing and celebrating people, and that's a sad but common occurrence. And if you find you're in a relationship like that, where you feel unseen and unheard and taken for granted, you're probably not going to turn that around by pointing fingers, and letting your partner know all the many ways he or she is blowing it, because it's never one person. In any relationship, there are two people, and the third thing, the space between them. That is where the relationship exists, in that space. Each person offers contributions to that space, and this is true whether we're speaking romantically or otherwise.

It's easy to lose the thread, but if there was a spark in the beginning, if there was communication and vulnerability and honesty, you can find those things again, by offering them yourself. When you change what you do, things change around you, people respond to you differently. Also, your happiness is your own responsibility. You can't put that on anyone else, that's an inside job. If you are not at peace within yourself, if you're not feeling inspired, if you're not loving yourself well, no one can solve that but you. The idea in a healthy relationship is that you support your partner, you don't look to him or her to solve your pain for you.

If you're in an abusive relationship, and by that I mean verbally, emotionally, or physically abusive, it's time to do something. Physical abuse demands that you create physical boundaries. In other words, you have to get out, and you'll definitely need support in doing that. You cannot stay and expect things to change, because they won't. Or they will, but not in a good way. Your life here is a gift. It isn't something you want to gamble. And thinking your love or patience or tolerance will finally change things is a dangerous delusion.

If we're talking about verbal and emotional abuse, boundaries are also in order. If you're not worried about your physical safety, it's time to draw the line in other areas. If a person cannot treat you with care and consideration, then what is the relationship about? Are you financially dependent? Does the abuse remind you of the way you grew up? Does some part of you believe that you are not good enough to deserve love? If you get a yes to any of those questions, you need help and support. Low self-esteem is dangerous because we betray ourselves when we feel we aren't worthy of being cherished. We put ourselves in situations that are crushing and heartbreaking, and you can only take that for so long before you become depressed or hardened, or you need to numb the pain. That's no way to live.

There is no happily ever after without your participation and action. There is no person who's going to sweep in and save the day and make everything okay, unless you decide to be that person. Be that person, seriously.

See the Pain Beneath the Words

Have you ever gone to see a film with a friend, and come out to discover you have two completely different viewpoints about what you've just seen? Obviously, it's not that you've seen two different movies, it's that you and your friend are bringing two different perspectives to a

31

shared experience. I think that's clear when we're in that context, but we seem to forget it's the same with life.

We're always bringing so much to the table. We have our life experiences, our histories, our opinions and feelings and things we've been taught, in addition to our current mood and circumstances. This is really helpful to remember when we find ourselves totally thrown by someone else's behavior or different take on a situation. It's also good to remember when we move through conflict with those we love.

So much of the time, we get caught up in the story, or our need to be right. If we're not seeing eye to eye with a loved one, we might expend a lot of energy trying to convince them to see things our way. We might dig our heels in, or shake our heads, or throw our hands in the air in our attempts to "win" a fight. But when we separate ourselves from those we love because being right is more important than being close, no one wins.

If, for example, your partner feels jealous, and you know in your heart there's no need for that fear, you might become impatient or angry or indignant. Maybe you try to reassure once or twice, but then you feel frustrated that you have to waste time and energy putting her or him at ease when you aren't doing anything wrong. You could take that tack, but you could also stop and breathe and consider your partner's life experiences. Maybe they've been betrayed in the past, more than once. Don't get me wrong, here. I'm not talking about pathological jealousy, or controlling or violating behavior. I'm not suggesting it's ever okay if the person you're with is checking your email or your text messages, or showing up unannounced. That kind of behavior chokes the life, trust and health out of any relationship.

What I'm talking about is clear communication and compassion. When we love people, we love the whole person, with all their beauty and all their flaws and occasional absurdities, just as we hope they'll also love us. We don't reject the challenging parts. We don't walk away when a person we love is in pain. One of the most loving things you can do for anyone is to try to understand their perspective, because underneath words and stories, there are always feelings. Sometimes in the middle of a charged exchange, it's incredibly revealing to stop listening to the words, and just look at your loved one's face. Maybe you're going to see fear or anger, because when we love, we make ourselves vulnerable, and when we feel threatened, it's human for us to want to protect what we love. Generally, if you can see the pain or fear beneath the words, it makes it so much easier to be kind and understanding. That's what we all want, right? To be seen and understood. To feel that if we've given someone our heart, we can trust that they'll take care of it, and that they won't shame us or reject us for our insecurities. We all have some, after all.

The other thing that's such a relief, and often comes with time and distance, is just the realization that so little is personal. We've all had our experiences and our life lessons, and most of us have learned at least a few things along the way that are not true. Like, maybe you learned that "everyone cheats", or "everyone leaves", because that's what you saw growing up, and that's what you've unconsciously sought out as an adult, in an effort to re-write your story. Maybe it just hasn't occurred to you yet, it isn't that everyone cheats, it's that all the people you've picked, cheat. Ugh. Not a very fun realization, but key for your healing and happiness.

Anyway, my point is, if you love someone, and I don't just mean romantically, part of your job is to help them unlearn anything that's blocking their happiness. I mean, you don't have to take that on, that's advanced love, but the option is there for you to be that person.

If you can really make those closest to you feel safe to be fully themselves, and to know that you won't walk away, you set the stage to be received in the same way. Not everyone is going to accept that invitation, but you don't need everyone, just a handful of people is a blessing. You can always have at least one person who accepts you entirely, because you always have the power to do that for yourself. And it's a relief, really. We all have our struggles, fears and pain. That doesn't make us less lovable.

When to Hold On, and When to Let Go

Sometimes it's so hard to know when to hold on, and when to let go. This comes up in all kinds of relationships. Often, we're dealing with people who simply do not know how to love. Maybe there's a history of abuse, and they're passing on what was done to them. Maybe there are personality disorders, and we're dealing with people who don't feel empathy, and are incapable of communicating in a compassionate way. There are people who go up and down--sometimes they're rational, and other times there's no logic at all, no possibility for understanding. Those are often the most challenging cases, because we get lulled when things are good, and blindsided when the tides turn. The thing is, after you've been through a few cycles with someone, you have to stop allowing yourself to think things are going to be okay every time they have a good week. Your heart is soft, and it can only take so much battering. Also, you are the steward of your own ship, and if you keep sailing into tsunamis, you can't expect things to go well. There are cases when we're dealing with betrayal, and it's hard to know if we should try to open again, or cut our losses and move on. Sometimes we've just grown in different directions and need something else, maybe something we've never known before, like belief in ourselves.

Here's the thing. If someone has a history of treating you badly, you have to distance yourself. I mean, if it's not a relationship you want to end completely, then boundaries are your only option. I'm talking about familial relationships here. Most people do not want to cut ties with their parents, siblings, or exes when there are children involved. I really consider that a last resort. There's a deep pain when we have to walk away from people who were meant to love us, and didn't or couldn't. There are cases when ending the relationship and cutting off ties is the only option, so I want to acknowledge that. But short of instances of abuse, boundaries will usually get the job done. We can love people who have a hard time being consistent, while still loving ourselves.

If your parent or parents have never been there for you, if you've had a fear-based relationship and doubted your value to them, I do think you need to step away. Sometimes that's incredibly difficult. If you rely on your parents financially, or you come from a culture where you don't leave home until you get married, it's not as easy as just moving out and starting your own life. Obviously, it's very hard to heal and to create guidelines when you're living under the same roof with people who've let you down in all the important ways. And you can recognize that perhaps your parents are repeating what was done to them, but that does not lessen the impact on your own gorgeous heart. It's beautiful if you can see that it isn't about you, or anything lacking within you. It takes strength and insight to understand that some people, even your parents, might not have the tools to love you well, and that it isn't a reflection on you. You're lovable. You're made of love and you're full of love, and if your own parents can't see that and receive that and embrace that and nurture that, that is very sad for them, and a heartbreak for you all. But that doesn't mean you can't or won't have love in your own life. I would say removing yourself from the situation is ideal, but if you aren't in a place where you can do that yet, protect your heart in all the ways you can. Nurture yourself, be kind to yourself. Mother yourself.

If we're talking about romantic relationships, betrayal is a tough one, and I also think it's a case-by-case situation. Let me say that if you are unhappy in the context of your committed relationship, bringing another party into the mix is a very bad idea. If there are children in the picture, you're putting your whole family on the line. You're also making troubled waters murkier. If you're at the point where you'd even consider going outside your relationship, it's time to grab your partner and head to therapy. Because the answers to the problems do not reside in a third party. That isn't going to fix things, it's going to confuse them further. Maybe you and your partner have gotten off track. Maybe you've dropped the thread. Maybe you're so convinced you know everything there is to know about one another, you don't even pay attention anymore. Perhaps you're out of balance. Maybe there are little ones in the picture, and you haven't figured out how to nurture them, keep a roof over your heads, and still find time for romance. Maybe you're full of rage or resentment, or a list of ways your partner isn't showing up for you. Maybe you've shut down. The things is, relationships need our time and attention. Human beings thrive on love and connection and communication.

Sometimes people blow it. They get desperate. They feel lonely or unseen or unheard, or they feel unwanted in every way, and they act. Maybe they've felt rejected or disrespected, and someone at work is making them feel amazing, like everything they say and do is brilliant, like they're hot and desirable and hilarious. You know how it goes. A flirtation starts to build and then there's emailing or texting and the next thing you know, something has happened. I mean, you can't play with fire like that and expect to walk away unharmed. But when there are other people in the mix, like your family, that hurt has deep and far-reaching consequences. And now, instead of focusing on the problems that existed between you and your partner, the number one priority will be fixing what you've done, if your partner is even open to allowing you to try. You're going to have to be patient, and understand you broke their trust. They might want to see your emails and texts for a good long while. You're going to have to be transparent, and also compassionate.

Basically, you've just created a bigger mess for yourself, and you're likely to feel resentful, because all the other issues are going to take a backseat to your making things right, which might not be possible. Having said that, people can recover from betrayal. It takes two people who are willing to fight for the relationship. If there are kids in the mix, I hope you try. If it's a pattern, and there's a history of cheating, you're probably not in a good situation. But if it's a one-time thing, and you can recognize that both parties contributed to the deterioration of the relationship prior to the betrayal, you can come out stronger on the other side.

Sometimes there are no kids in the picture, but there's a long partnership. People sometimes write in and ask if it's okay to leave someone just because they feel pulled to do so. Usually, these are people who are very used to putting other people's feelings, needs and wants ahead of their own. I don't believe anyone would thank you for staying in a situation out of pity or guilt. We all deserve more than that, don't you think? It's never easy knowing what to do when our heart is in the mix, and other people are involved. I do think people tend to walk away from their families too easily these days. I think it's heartbreaking when parents and children don't speak, when brothers and sisters aren't in contact, when people leave the families they've started without giving it everything they've got, first. But I also think life is a miracle, and we don't have time to waste. If you know a thing is dead, release yourself, and the other party. If you're holding on to something toxic, by all means let go, or get yourself help doing that if you need it. Love is worth fighting for, and sometimes that means we hold on, and sometimes it means we let go.

How's Your Side of the Street?

If you have some idea that you can save people, or make another person feel happy or whole or healed, you're setting yourself up for disappointment, and maybe worse. Wanting to help people is beautiful; we could use more of that in the world. That impulse is the catalyst that leads someone to share, to listen, to offer support or encouragement. But thinking that you can swoop in and make things right for someone who's in pain, just with the depth of your love and concern, is a recipe for disaster.

I say this whether we're talking about your best friend, your new friend, your child, your parent, your partner, or your new romantic interest. Each of us must do our own work. And sometimes when we try to make things right for someone, we unintentionally rob them of an experience that might have helped them grow. But it's brutal to watch someone we love suffer. It's natural to want to comfort and nurture, and if you can see a clear path toward happiness, of course you want to point the way. It's fine to offer tools that have worked for you if they're open to your ideas, but people do things as they're ready. You can't micro-manage someone else's journey.

Furthermore, when we spend lots of time and energy focused on what someone else is, or is not doing, saying, or being, we conveniently stop paying attention to our own growth, our own needs, our own healing. And honestly, we all have work enough to do, just keeping our own side of the street clean. Life asks us to rise up every day, to show up and be present, to listen, to reflect, to respond, to engage. You have this one life, and what you do with it is up to you. But if you allow years to go by where you're so caught up in someone else's life that you forget to live your own, that's time you'll never have back.

Sometimes you have to ask yourself if you want a partner, or a project. If you grew up thinking that love had to be earned, and that it could be taken away if you didn't measure up, you probably have a lot of work to do in your current relationships, romantic or otherwise. When we don't value ourselves, we gravitate toward people to whom we might become invaluable. "I'll just be perfect for this person, I'll give them everything they need, and then they won't leave me or hurt me or betray me." That isn't love, that's a project.

When our children are young, we have to lean over the plate and cut the pancakes, or halve the grapes, or put lids on the cups so everything doesn't spill down the front of these people we love. But if you find yourself metaphorically doing these things for grown adults, whether they're your children or your friends, something is off.

Try to get very clear on what you want. If you want love and peace in your life, you won't find those things by trying to control other people, or circumstances. Love can't exist in a vise grip, because love needs room to move and expand. Try to trust enough to allow for that expansion.

You Can't Negotiate with Crazy

People can only drive us crazy if we let them. A person can spin his or her web, but we don't have to fly into the center of it to be stunned, stung, paralyzed and eaten. Remember that your time and your energy are the most precious gifts you have to offer anyone, and that includes those closest to you, and also total strangers. Your energy and your time are also both finite. So it's really important to be mindful about where you're placing those gifts.

It's hard not to get caught up when someone we love is suffering, or thrashing around, or in so much pain they don't know what else to do but lash out. It's hard not to take that to heart, or to defend yourself, or to try to make things better for them. But you're not going to walk into a ring and calm a raging bull with your well-thought out dialogue. You're just going to get kicked in the face, at best. And I use that analogy intentionally. People in pain—whether we're talking about people with personality disorders or clinical depression, people suffering with addiction, or people who are going through mind-boggling loss—are dealing with deep and serious wounds. They didn't wake up this way one morning. Whether it's a chronic issue, or an acute and immediate situation, when you're dealing with heightened emotions including rage, jealousy, or debilitating fear, you're not going to help when a person is in the eye of the storm. If someone is irrational, trying to reason with them makes you as irrational as they are. You can't negotiate with crazy. And I'm not using the word as a dagger. I'm saying we're all crazy sometimes. We're all beyond reason sometimes. We all have days when we feel everyone is against us, whether that's based in any kind of reality or not.

You can offer your love, your patience, your kindness and your compassion if someone you care for is suffering. You can try to get them the support they need. You can make them a meal, or show up and just be there to hold their hand, or take them to the window to let in a little light. But if someone is attacking you verbally or otherwise, we're in a different territory. You are not here to be abused, mistreated, or disrespected. You are not here to defend yourself against someone's need to make you the villain. You don't have to give that stuff your energy, and I'd suggest that you don't. It's better spent in other places.

We can lose hours and days and weeks getting caught up in drama or someone else's manipulation. That's time we'll never have back. Of course things happen in life; people do and say and want things that can be crushing sometimes. But the real story to examine is always the story of our own actions. If someone needs you to be the bad guy, why do you keep trying to prove you're actually wonderful? Are you wonderful? Brilliant, get back to it! If someone has a mental illness and they are incapable of controlling themselves, keeping their word, or treating you with respect, why do you keep accepting their invitation to rumble? You already know what's going to happen. Don't you have a better way to spend your afternoon? My point is, life is too short.

When a person is in the kind of pain that causes them to create pain around them, your job is to create boundaries if it's someone you want to have in your life. You figure out how to live your life and honor your own well-being, and deal with the other party in a way that creates the least disharmony for you. That means you don't take the bait when they put their dukes up. You don't allow yourself to get sucked in. Do you really think this is the time you'll finally be heard or seen or understood? People who need to be angry cannot hear you. It doesn't matter what you do or say, they have a construct they've built to support a story about their life that they can live with; it doesn't have to be based in reality. Not everyone is searching for their own truth or their own peace; some people are clinging to their rage, because that feels easier or more comfortable, or because they really, truly aren't ready to do anything else yet. You're not going to solve that. But you can squander your time and energy trying. You can make yourself sick that way. I just don't recommend it.

You really don't have to allow other people to steal your peace, whether we're talking about those closest to you, or people you don't even know, like the guy who cuts you off on the freeway, or the woman talking loudly on her cellphone at the bank. You don't have to let this stuff get under your skin and agitate you. You don't have to let someone's thoughtless comment or action rob you of a beautiful afternoon. You can always come back to center, and breathe.

CHAPTER 3: ATTACHMENT

Most of us have our ideas about how things should be, and how life should look and what other people should want and need. And that "should" really gets us into trouble. Attachment leads to suffering. We can't control circumstances or other people's desires, any more than we can control the tides of the ocean. It's always better to dive in, and just figure out which way to swim.

The Full Range of Motion of Your Heart

When my son was six, he fell off the jungle gym at school on Halloween morning and broke his elbow. He was in a cast for a month, and when you're an active, six-year old kid, that feels like an eternity. On the afternoon I took my kids to the orthopedist to have the cast removed, it was like Christmas morning. We were all really excited that he was "getting his arm back." When the cast came off, he looked at his arm. The skin was very dry and peeling in places. It hadn't seen the light of day in a month, after all. When the nurse left the room, my son looked at me with his brow furrowed and very quietly said, "I thought it was going to look normal." I could tell he was trying not to cry. I explained that we are all shedding skin all the time, and that the skin on his arm would be back to normal in no time. I also told him it was fine to cry, but that he didn't need to worry. He also discovered that he couldn't make a fist yet, or fully bend or straighten his arm. For the rest of that day, he carried his arm as if the cast was still on it. He did his homework with his right hand for the first time in a month, but other than that, he continued to use his left arm.

Anyway, all of this got me thinking about expectations, and also about times we feel compressed or restricted, and what happens when we're finally free. There are few things more likely to land us in a world of trouble than our own expectations of how things should be, or how other people should feel or behave, or how life should look (expectations tend to keep the company of the word "should", and whenever I find myself using that word I stop and check in. There are only a few places the word "should" isn't dangerous. Like, everyone should floss. Or, people should pick up after their dogs).

When walking into a situation, whether it be a new job, a party at a friend's house, or new a relationship, I really believe the two best things to be are curious, and breathing consciously. The minute we unpack a bunch of our expectations all over a circumstance, we deny ourselves and anyone else involved the possibility of just being present, open and aware. We lose the chance to explore and figure out, with open eyes, whether this is the kind of situation that is going to bring us love, growth, and fulfillment, or whether it really doesn't feel right. Sometimes we get attached to an outcome and breeze right by the fact that our heart is saying, "No, this is not the way." I think a lot of this comes from our desire to control things. If we can predict the future based on the past, it becomes less uncertain. And most humans suffer from fear of the unknown to some degree or another.

The thing is, the whole future is unknown. We really don't know what will happen in our lives in the next ten minutes, hours, days, weeks, years. We can't predict that or control it. Having intentions is great. Knowing yourself, and uncovering what it is that lights you up, and committing to spreading your gifts wherever you go is beautiful, but expecting life to unfold in a particular way is a set-up. You set yourself up to feel disappointed if it doesn't look like the picture in your head, and life rarely does. Sometimes it brings more beauty and joy than you ever could have imagined, and other times it breaks your heart wide open and hands you the kind of devastation that leaves you working to just breathe. We may as well open to what is, and face the reality that everything is always changing, and that one day we will all exhale for the last time, so there's nothing to do but get busy living, growing, accepting, and surrendering to the beauty and the pain.

The other thing is that cast. It reminded me of times in my life when I've felt restricted or compressed. When I've allowed my light to be dimmed for any number of reasons. You can get used to compression; it can become your "new normal." I was considering the pain of that, because it requires complicity. Nothing and no one can dim your light unless you allow that to happen, unless you take part in that dimming. You won't do that when you're loving yourself, but when you're in pain, you might. Digging your way out of that kind of darkness is not easy, because it requires that you look at your end. You examine why you took part in the crushing of your own soul. Those are important questions, and you need the answers in order to heal, and move forward, and carry the light in your heart as the miraculous gift that it is. Your offering is precious because no one can offer it but you.

The funny thing is, once you step outside into the light, you might not know exactly what to do with yourself at first. Your soul may need a minute to realize the cast has come off. A moment to expand, to reach out, to flex its muscle and start shining again. The full range of motion of your heart is mind-blowing. Your soul on fire is a feeling you don't want to miss. See if you can drop your expectations and expand fully in every direction, but give yourself time, and have compassion. This business of being human is not easy, and the path to opening is similar to that very first path to opening we all endure—it's dark and the way is not always clear, and as we struggle toward the light we get squeezed and eventually we come out and take that huge inhale. And then we wail. And then with love and a lot of help we figure it out. Life is a constant opportunity for rebirth, for breathing, and for helping each other along the way.

Make Your Art

This is pretty much how I feel about life. Every day we're granted is a chance to make art. The art of living life with your heart open. The art of moving from, and with love. The art of healing yourself, of listening deeply, of giving whatever you've got to spread some light, some joy, some laughter. The art of a great hug. The art of creating a space where healing is likely to occur, for yourself, and for as many other people as you can. Some of the most beautiful art I know, is the art of being present. Of giving someone your time, your attention, access to your soul. Everyone deserves that. To be truly seen, heard, experienced.

You won't always succeed, but treating your life and the way you're living it as your canvas, and painting it with every gorgeous color in your soul is the only way I know to make the art you're here to share. Worrying about how you'll be received or perceived is all too human, but it's also a complete waste of your resources. Trying to please everyone is exhausting and impossible, and it's also a sure-fire way to cut yourself off from your inspiration, your yes, your divine spark. If you make your art from a place of love, you really can't go wrong. You may not please every-one, but as long as you aren't intentionally hurting anyone (I'm not talking about those times when we will all inevita-bly hurt people because we've grown in a different direc-tion. I'm talking about indifference to someone else's well-being, feelings, situation, heart), you have to shine your light. You have to dip your brush in the well of what is true for you, and splash the stuff that lights you up from within, all over your canvas.

It is not your job to convince anyone that your art is worthwhile or important or good. It's not your job to wipe someone else's lenses and sell them on how awesome you are. You are supposed to be awesome. You're no different than the sun, or the ocean, or the bella luna. You're part of all of that, with some stardust splashed in, too. There is nothing to prove. There are just many incredible and obvi-ous things to be: curious, loving, open, attentive, laughing, grateful, awake, amazed.

That's your light, and you're meant to shine it. You're meant to uncover it and share it and spread it everywhere you go. We need to feel that connection to what is true for us, and the joy in life comes from the sharing of it. Of course it is extra special to be received with love. But you are love, so you can do that for yourself, too.

Some people will come and share some of their art on your canvas in this life if you let them. And you will some-times paint on someone else's also. If you have children one day, you will want them to finger paint all over your stuff until they find their own canvas. Sometimes in life someone's art complements our own so well, we decide to share a space to shine, and sometimes the art moves in two different directions.

If at all possible, celebrate the process of making it, and try not to worry too much about whether it's turning out the way you envisioned. Maybe you'll surprise yourself. Maybe some color will come out of you that you never knew existed. Be bold. Be willing to get messy. Try not to be disturbed when every color coming out of you is dark. If you looked back on the canvases of the most happy people you know, I guarantee somewhere you'd find the midnight blue of despair. The dark grey of loneliness. The muddy brown of confusion. The blackness of fear. And splashes of those shadow colors throughout the entire piece. How else would you see the extraordinary light if not for the darker hues? Because this work of being human is messy and complicated. Sometimes it will break your heart, and sometimes your broken heart will open in ways that create the most piercingly beautiful colors. It is all gorgeous and necessary and worthwhile. It is all your art. And it is stunning, just like you.

And just so you know, you can come paint on my canvas anytime. Sending you so much love, and flicking a little paint at you, too.

The Double-Edged Sword of Attachment

Recently, my dear old dad was visiting from North Carolina. I don't see him as much as I'd like to because of the distance, but we make the most of the time we have, and the visits are frequent enough that my kids know and adore their grandpa. They're also infrequent enough that he really sees the leaps in growth for both kids, and I notice the changes he's going through acutely, as well.

On this last trip, we went to the beach. It was a hot day, and I knew my kids would love to swim in the ocean and build sandcastles, and I figured my dad wouldn't mind sticking his toes in the water, either. My dad is eighty-eight. He's got the brainpower he's always had, but the body is slowing down. He also spent years running six miles a day on the streets of New York City, so the knees are not what they once were. But he works out every morning, looks fit and strong, and still has that spark in his eye.

Anyway, we drove to the beach instead of walking, because I knew the hill on the way home would be too much. Also, he'd just talked to me about the particulars of his will, and other things he thought I ought to know about his wishes when the time comes. That's where we're at now. It's not some conceptual thing that might happen in the distant future, it's a reality, and we both know it. I mean, my great Aunt Tess lived to 103 years old, and was sharp as a whip until her final exhale, so I'm not counting him out. It's just, you have to start to accept the inevitable at some point. We don't last in the bodies we have forever and ever. And we'll all be lucky if we make it to eighty-eight. It's not like we can ever take anything for granted, including tomorrow. But we do it all the time. So anyway, we drove to the beach.

When we got there, I laid out a blanket, and my kids took off for the water. My dad and I followed. He was wearing shorts, not a bathing suit, so we went knee-deep, but the waves were splashing and he was getting a little wetter than he wanted, so we decided to back up a little. When my dad turned around, he lost his footing and couldn't recover, and I watched him fall onto his side. I could see he was upset and disconcerted and maybe even a little afraid. I wasn't sure if I should reach out and pull him up, or let him get up on his own, because he also seemed embarrassed. I'd have to guess it's a difficult thing to have your body betray you, and to have yourself laid out in front of your kid. But the waves kept coming and the sand was soft and uneven, and I could see that he needed help to get up, and that he was willing to receive it, so I put my hands under his arms like I've done for my kids a million times, and we got him back to standing. I could feel his heart racing and his body shaking.

He held onto my arm until we were back on the blanket. When I sat down next to him, he said, "Well, that was my act for the day." And he told me that his balance has been off since he had emergency pacemaker surgery a few years ago. I was grateful neither of my kids had seen, because I think they would have been scared. For me, I just felt sad. My dad has never been a "false bravado" kind of guy; he's always been honest with me about his struggles, and when I was little, it was way too much. I know he has regrets about that. I see the way he is with my kids, and I know if he had some things to do over again as a father, he'd do them differently. I also know he loves me to pieces. We've been through all that, and have nothing left to clear up, which is a gift and a relief. You don't want to feel you've left things unsaid or unresolved. My dad of today is not my dad of yesteryear.

I think this is an important point, because so many people get stuck in a time warp and feed their rage, which doesn't leave any room for change or growth, and doesn't allow the space for something new to emerge. You are not the same you of last year, and a year from now, the you you are today will have evolved and shifted in ways you can't imagine. The same is true for anyone. I know so many people who are grown adults, still blaming their parents for their unhappiness.

Here's the reality: some people should not have children because they don't have the emotional tools, patience, maturity and resilience for it. That doesn't mean you have to hate them for it for all eternity, and it doesn't mean you shouldn't be here, shining in all your glory. It just means you may have some serious work to do to get from there to here. So that's your work. Is that "fair"? No. It's just what is, and you might as well deal with it, and get yourself whatever support you need to work it out, because figuratively, it won't be that long before you've fallen in the ocean and can't get up.

I think the main thing is to live your life in a way that you can feel at peace about it when you're eighty-eight. We are all going to make mistakes, some huge and some small. The best thing I know to do is to acknowledge the mistakes when you make them, to examine what happened that resulted in your not showing up the way you wanted to, so you can do it differently the next time. It's not about not making mistakes, it's about making better mistakes as you go. And also, you can always try to mend fences when possible. Not everyone will be open to forgiveness. You can't force it, and if someone won't meet you halfway, that's how it is. But change does happen and some people do learn, and do shift, and do want to fix things and grow beauty out of pain. I'm not saying you have to let them. Some things are unforgivable. There are certainly instances where you have to create and maintain boundaries for your own well-being. But those are extreme cases.

Lastly, we should all remember to say what's in our hearts. Sometimes it's tempting to think we can wait until it feels easier, or to put things off because we're busy or immersed in our own lives. But you can't take anyone for granted, at any age. The vulnerability of being human is just built into the experience. Fighting that, denying it, or ignoring it won't make it go away, it'll just exhaust you. Better to open your heart, your hands and your mind, and love the people in your life with everything you've got. Better to have the hard conversations that touch the raw places so you create an environment where healing can occur. Better to slow down, and appreciate the beauty, the gifts and the love, because they don't last forever.

The Picture in Your Head

Do you know people who get married because they're thirty and the clock is ticking, and that's where they thought they'd be by thirty, and so this guy or girl will have to be the one? Or talk to people with rigid ideas about things, like, if they're dating someone for a year and there's no ring, it's over? How about people who go to medical school because that's what their dad did and their grandfather, too, and that's just what people in their family do? When you have a picture in your head about how something should look or feel, you are rejecting things (or people) as they are. Sometimes the person you reject is you, your authentic self.

Life rarely looks the way we thought it would. Sometimes it's so much more incredible than what we had imagined, and other times it's way more painful than we had hoped. But there are always opportunities to grow and to open, to dig more deeply and see more clearly. I don't know why things unfold the way they do. I have theories and ideas like we all do, but who knows if they're right? Some things are so incomprehensibly painful you just have to let your heart be broken open.

Whatever your feelings, the ability to embrace reality

makes the journey so much easier. Try to draw a huge heart around all of it, and make it big enough that life still has room to surprise you. Look at your life as it is, with curiosity and compassion for yourself and everyone you encounter, because it's not an easy thing, this business of being human. To be awake and aware and engaged with what is, not with a daydream or a fantasy or a memory or a picture in your head. I'm not saying thoughts aren't powerful. The chair you're sitting on started as a thought in someone's head. I'm just saying, don't think your way into a box, where nothing but the picture you've imagined will do, because it might not go like that.

I had a beautiful birth plan with my first, for example. Low lights, no drugs, just a few people to support me. I ended up with a respiratory team in the room, monitors blaring, fear like I've never known before or since, panic everywhere. But you know what? I have the most amazing son. Like, insanely amazing. Kind and sweet and smart and funny with a smile that could light up any room. He has incredible enthusiasm for life, hunger for information, a contagious laugh. There's more love than my heart can hold. So much laughter, so many hugs, such an adventure. And we are both okay. And there has been more joy than I ever pictured or imagined or planned for. Open to what is. Be with it. Explore it. Maybe you'll be surprised, amazed, heartbroken, head over heels in love. I don't know. But I do know that whatever you take in as it is, is real, is full of truth, and its own particular beauty, even if it's the truth and beauty of having your heart broken. This is the ride, this is the best mode of transportation I know. The rest of it is numbed out illusion, a dream, a sleepwalk, an attempt to control something that is really no different than if you woke up today and decided you were going to try to manipulate the weather. Just grab your bathing suit or your umbrella, and make the most of it.

Where Are You Rooted?

Yesterday my six year old son asked me if I knew about the "walking palm trees of the rainforest." He told me that these trees were able to "move their roots" if they saw a spot that looked better to them. I told him that was incredibly cool, and that I did not know about these trees. Of course, I had to go Google it, because palm trees walking around the rainforest seems like something I'd have heard about somewhere along the way.

So it turns out the Socratea exorrhiza, or, "Walking Palm" is native to tropical Central and South America, and it has stilt roots that allow it to grow in swampy areas of forest. Some people think their roots exist as an adaptation to flooding, and others believe the roots allow the palm to "walk away" if another tree falls on the seedling and knocks it over. If this happens, the palm produces new vertical stilt roots and rights itself, the original roots rotting away.

I think life asks us to do this very thing again and again; to start over, to respond to the ever-changing nature of things, to move our roots when we need to, and right ourselves. But a lot of the time, we resist. We cling to the dying roots that don't sustain us or nurture us anymore, that cannot support our growth any longer. Sometimes we do this out of desperation. We love someone, or many "someones" and can't bear the thought of hurting them, or we're afraid of all that is required to pick up and move toward the unknown. In relationships, it's incredibly painful. The roots grow down directly from our hearts. But if you aren't growing, you're dying, and if you're dying, you can't nurture anyone else because all your energy is going toward your withering and quiet destruction. Without living, healthy roots, you just won't have the strength to rise up and reach the light. And so life becomes very dark, indeed.

I know so many people who keep feeding those dying roots, though. It's all swampy and murky, and nothing new can grow there, but still, they try to shore the thing up, to feed it whatever they can. Sometimes it's old stories that have become rooted. They're poisoning the tree, the branches are hanging low, the leaves have mostly fallen off, but the roots of blame or anguish or fear or sadness, of bitterness or shame or guilt, keep the person rooted in the Forest of What Was. I spent a good decade in that forest, so I can tell you the main thing that grows there are weeds. The kind that climb up your trunk and strangle your branches and steal all the light and all the nutrients, until you are just this Tree of Blame with sour fruit. "I am this way because this happened, and then that happened, and then this other thing happened, and so now when you say you love me I don't believe you because everybody leaves and everybody cheats and I'm just going to stay rooted here in the darkness." Or something like that.

Fear will keep you paralyzed in that forest if you let it. But it's such a shame, because old stories are old, they don't have to control your present or your future. They may have created some grooves in your trunk, but they don't have to overtake your ability to produce the sweetest fruit you can imagine; the fruit of, "I Got the F&ck Out!!!", for example. That is some sweet fruit. You may feel stuck and powerless. You may even be rooted to those feelings; there may be some pay-off for you in staying stuck. Attachment to sympathy or attention, a reason not to do the brave and difficult thing so you can stick with what you know even if it doesn't feel good, or an excuse to numb out are some possibilities. But I have to let you know, the pay-off of digging deep, to the very bottom of your soul, gathering up your courage and your stilt roots, and moving your ass to the Forest of Life is Freaking Amazing, has much greater rewards. If a tree can do it, I have zero doubt you can do it, too, if you haven't already. Sending you a shovel and a gentle nudge if you need one!

Let Go or Be Dragged (Zen Proverb)

Sometimes we're so attached to an idea, it blinds us. Maybe we're in love with someone, and we so want them to be in love with us, too, we deny the nagging feeling that it doesn't seem to be the case. We think if we chase, or hang in there, or show up exactly the way we think this person wants us to, then it will work out, then we'll "have" them. We start to try to fit in to some kind of mold. We obsess and doubt and worry about everything, and we lose ourselves.

Attachment ("raga") is one of the five "kleshas", or obstacles that prevent us from experiencing oneness, that deep sense of being in the flow that Patanjali lays out in the second chapter of the Yoga Sutras. That, to me, is the real peace. The surrender, in the bravest sense, to what is, and the ability to open to it and join in it. Some of it is very painful, and not at all as we'd like it to be, and some of it is so piercingly beautiful, it takes your breath away. The work is to hold it all, embrace it all, even when you don't understand. Recognizing that you are not in control of circumstances, or other people, or the way the story will unfold. Letting go of your grip on things. That's the good kind of "losing yourself." What you get to work on is your response to what you're given, your ability to return to love again and again, even if your heart is broken.

The other four obstacles are ignorance ("avidya", a disconnection from what's real, an inability to see things clearly), egoism ("asmita", identification with our ideas about ourselves, our judgments and "shoulds"), aversion ("dvesha", a rejection of, or desire to avoid those things that are unwanted, whether they be particular feelings, reality as it is unfolding, other people, a certain outcome, or a way of being), and fear of death ("abhinivesha", the fear of loss, fear of the unknown, fear that we will leave important things unsaid or undone).

The yoga practice is about stripping away those obstacles. When we're attached to a particular outcome, we close off the possibility for anything else. We stand there with our eyes shut tightly, gripping onto our vision of how we want things to be. And anything that doesn't fit into our picture must be rejected or denied. But when you reject reality, you leave yourself in a world of darkness, you become the architect of your own suffering. If you want to know which way to go, you have to open your eyes, because there's nothing to follow but the truth. And when I say that, I mean the truth of each moment, the truth of your particular situation, the truth that's in your heart. When you start following those truths, you pave the way to experience the bigger truth of your connection to everything, your part in the flow.

When I started practicing yoga, I was a person who was trying to chase happiness. If I just do this or that, then I'll be happy. "This" might be meeting the right person. "That" might be losing just a little more weight, or nine million other things that all had to do with external stuff. I had this idea that happiness was somewhere out in front of me, and that it would present itself if I just worked hard and made it to certain milestones. But when you live your life that way, you begin to understand that's all a lie. You hit the milestone, and it's still not enough. Happiness is never outside of you. It's inside. And it's not something you need to create, it's something that's already there, just waiting to be uncovered.

The stripping away process can be painful. It can sear you a little, or a lot. You may have to burn away all kinds of beliefs about yourself and other people, about the world and your part in it. But the gift of yoga, if you practice long enough, is that it makes you hungry for the truth, whatever it is. Even if it's painful. Even if you have to face a reality you'd do anything to avoid. When you're in love with someone and they aren't in love with you, somewhere deep down you know that, you feel it. That's what makes you feel sick and doubtful and hooked in that awful way. You're blinding yourself to reality. You're cutting yourself off from your own intuition. So you might go through some pain, but eventually there's a real liberation when you just open your hands and your heart and your mind to the truth, whatever it may be. The truth burning away in your heart. The acceptance of someone else's truth, even if it means you must let go of some vision you had.

It's a liberation because it's exhausting to push down what you know. It's like trying to hold back the waves of the ocean; it simply cannot be done. When you accept that, you can relax and swim, you can be in and of the flow. And then you can devote your energy to living each day fully, to loving each person in your life fully, to sharing your gifts freely, with abandon. To leaving nothing unsaid or undone, so that if it were your last day (and I hope you have countless days ahead of you), you could end it with the sense of having done all you could today, to live with your heart wide open.

CHAPTER 4: SEEING CLEARLY

So much of the time, we suffer because we refuse to accept what's in front of our faces. There are all kinds of ways we lie to ourselves, deny reality, or try to blur the edges so things don't hurt as much, but that isn't living, that's existing. To live, you have to dig your hands into the heart of the matter and hold it up to the light. You can't hide from yourself or other people and expect to be happy. You can't create a false reality and demand that other people live in it. I mean, you can, but I don't think it'll go very well for you. Wiping our lenses clean, picking ourselves up, and seeing things as they are is the key to our liberation and peace.

The Danger of Shiny Packaging

Recently, I was at the grocery store with my kids, and my son asked if he could have a green juice he saw on the shelf. It was made by a company with shiny packaging, that purports to be all about good health, and natural ingredients. I pulled it down and looked at the back of the bottle, and my eyes popped out of my head: 53 grams of sugar. Even my son, who's eight, did not need an explanation about why we weren't going to buy it. Instead, we talked about critical thinking and not taking things at face value. And then we went home and made our own green juice.

The juice got me to thinking about a friend of mine who's going through some heartbreak. She was dating a man for the last eight months. Kind of a whirlwind thing, and also a case of good packaging. They moved in together after eight weeks of heated dating, and she was sure he was "the one." He was charming and kind and attentive and great-looking, and it seemed they had a good thing going. Until one of our mutual friends called to tell her he was active on Tinder, and had tried to make a date with her. So now my friend is crashing at her parents' house and looking for a place to live, and beating herself up.

The thing is, most of us have done this, romantically or otherwise. We make quick decisions based on how things look or seem, but when it comes to people, or situations, or even juice, you really have to take your time. Not everything is as it appears to be.

Some of the things that cloud our vision the most are our own wants, projections and assumptions. If you're longing for connection, for example, and you meet someone who's attractive to you, you may find yourself diving in and projecting all these wonderful traits on a person you really don't know. You don't know someone after a week, or two, or even six. If we're talking about romance, you really don't know, because nothing blinds us like hormones. You have to wait for the lust/dust to clear a little before you have any sense of who you're dealing with, and even then, it takes time.

Also, most people can do the beginning of relationships well. I mean, it's not hard, right? Spending time with someone you're nuts about, getting naked, and having lots of great sex? Not too many people are going to feel burdened or challenged by that! And those long conversations deep into the night, when neither of you cares about having to get up early in the morning. The touch of his hand, the look in her eye, the flirty texts. Even people who have a deep fear of intimacy can usually do the beginning pretty well. You know why, right? It's not really intimate yet. You can get physically naked with someone and not really know who they are. You can confide your past disappointments, your struggles, your fears, your hopes and your dreams, glossing over the darker stuff, and still not know someone, not deeply. Most people lead with their best foot. Most people are not going to tell you about their most challenging issues in the beginning, because they are digging the high off your adoration, just like you're digging the high off theirs. No one wants to burst that bubble. We all like to have a clean slate, a chance to begin again, an opportunity to see ourselves the way this new person is seeing us.

You get to know people slowly, whether we're talking about new friends, or romantic partners. Of course we love to pin things down and make our plans and think about the future, and that's okay, that's human. But the truth is, we never know what's coming next, and the best thing any of us can do is know ourselves, and stay centered. You don't have to decide how you feel about everything right off the bat. You can give yourself a little breathing room, and allow things, people, and situations to unfold. You don't have to decide "this is it!", and you don't have to decide "this isn't it." You can just enjoy and pay attention and see.

"Viveka", or discernment, is a huge part of the yoga practice. Recognizing what is real from what is not real, what is permanent versus what is impermanent. Solitude is part of being human. You'll spend more time with your internal dialogue, occupying the vast world of your innermost space, than you will with anyone else. People will only have access to that interior world to the extent that you allow, and the same holds true for others. You will only know anyone to the degree that they give you access. Some people guard the deepest sanctuary of their inner world out of fear. It might be fear of rejection, it might be fear of intimacy, it might be the fear of losing one's freedom. The point is, people are complicated, therefore situations involving people are doubly complicated. We all bring so much to the mix, and most of it is not on the surface. There are mysteries everywhere. To think you can figure it all out by skimming the top is a sure way to get bitten in the ass, and probably hard. Take your time with people. And take your time with juice, too.

Not This, Not That

In yoga practice, so much of what we're doing is about stripping away. It's very possible, and quite common, to reach adulthood and have no clue who we are or what we need to be at peace. Culturally we're taught to look outward for happiness. If we just meet certain "markers", if we can look right and have the right job and the right partner and the right house and car, then we'll be good to go. And a lot of people are so focused on attaining these outer signs of happiness, they pass right by the signs that would actually lead them there.

Also, there's the way you grew up. Maybe you were taught, in word or through actions, that your worth as a human being was based on your performance. If you did well in school, if you were a good boy or girl, then all would be well, but if you screwed up or failed to reach the bar, love was withdrawn and the disapproval was palpable. Maybe punishment was swift and intense. That's just one example, of course. There are many. Maybe you grew up in a house where you felt unsafe, and you learned to be indispensable or invisible depending on the moment. Maybe you were spoiled rotten and taught that you were the center of everything, and that other people existed in order to orbit around your needs and wants. And perhaps you were taught that your needs and wants were something you were supposed to swallow, and that your fears and dreams had very little impact on the world around you. Maybe you were parentified and got a huge lesson in care-taking and people-pleasing. It's a huge spectrum, but the chances for knowing yourself are slim in any of these scenarios.

This is why we have so many people who reach adulthood and have no idea which way to turn. The house doesn't do it, the diet doesn't do it, the right partner doesn't do it. What's the point? Where have they gone wrong, why isn't the formula working? The formula doesn't work because it's based on the stuff around us, not the stuff within us. I know someone who's been searching for the "perfect house" for years. Money isn't an issue. The location could be anywhere. But no matter where he goes or what kind of house he buys, it's never the right one. It never does the trick. If you want to be at peace, you have to get your true house in order. Your body is your home. If things are not well within you, they won't be well around you, even if you buy a mansion in Bali and have people on hand to feed you fresh mango at your every whim. There's no escaping yourself.

So in yoga, we're looking for "vidya" or "clear-seeing." Being able to identify what is real from what is unreal, what is permanent from what is impermanent. And you have to question everything you think you know, because you may have accepted things along the way, decades ago, that turn out not to be true for you. And you may have adopted ways of being that don't serve you, that disempower you, or block you from receiving love and joy. You may have a lot of unlearning to do. Maybe you've come to believe you aren't lovable, or that you're broken in some un-fixable way. Maybe you think you can't trust anyone, or everyone lies and cheats. There are all kinds of ideas you might have developed that just aren't true. And so you have to dig. You have to unearth. You have to do the work to heal your deepest wounds so they don't direct your entire life. The way to peace is inside, not outside. And the sooner you start, the faster you get to a place where life feels good. Avoiding this work is the surest way to suffer. And you aren't here to suffer, although it's part of life sometimes. You're here to shine. I wouldn't wait.

Swim with the Fishes

Sometimes what we think we know prevents us from seeing clearly. In, "Making a Friend of the Unknown", a talk by one of my favorite poets, David Whyte, he shares about how he studied zoology and marine biology before he dedicated himself to writing full-time. And he went to the Galapagos Islands, and got in the water with the fish, and he said he was very disappointed to discover the animals had not read the same books he had. And that they had "lives of their own." Awesome, right?

Our ideas and opinions and frame of reference color all of our experiences. We like to think we have things figured out, and we know all there is to know about the people closest to us. Did it ever occur to you that your mother has a libido, and this is one of the reasons you exist? I'm not suggesting you have to dwell on your mother's sexual drive, I'm just saying, do you think of your mother as a complete woman, with a life and feelings and mysteries all her own, heartbreaks you may know nothing about, secret hopes, dreams, longings, or do you have her in this box labeled "mom"?

We make snap judgments all the time. And let's get clear on this-- judgements are not bad, the mind is a tool of judgement. You pull up to a red light and make a judgement to stop your car. It's pre-judging that gets us into trouble, and yet we're so used to categorizing everything. We're taking in so much information all the time, but we're also missing so much. Maybe we see someone with a yoga mat slung over her shoulder and we think, "She's like me", or we notice someone's cool tattoo, or their smile, or the way they're carrying themselves and we think, "confident", "charismatic." Do you know a lot of sociopaths have those characteristics? I'm just saying.

I've been teaching so long at this point, mostly the room is full of people I know, with new faces showing up all the time, and I love that. It's rare for me to deal with a room full of people I don't know, who don't know me, unless I'm traveling to teach a workshop somewhere. But sometimes in those instances, I can feel the energy in the room. The withholding, the resistance, the pause before the judgement. "Am I going to like this? Am I going to be happy I chose to spend my afternoon this way? Am I going to sweat? Is it only going to be about whether I sweat?" The mind is constantly pulling us out of our experience so we can make decisions about the experience we're having. But the minute you label how you're feeling, you aren't feeling it anymore, you're thinking.

My mother today is not the mother of my childhood, and my father today is not the same father I grew up with. People change and things change but sometimes our ideas do not change along with them. I'm not the same teacher I was ten years ago, nor do I want to be. We're always learning and growing, and hopefully we're allowing life to open us and strengthen us so we have more to give. But we stunt that process when we place our ideas and opinions all over everything. It's like a grid or a screen we can't see through. We've decided things have to be one way, and we reject anything that doesn't match our vision.

The more you can drop what you think you know, and just open to things as they are, the less you'll struggle. Moving through life and interacting with people with curiosity is such a great way to go. We aren't here to pigeonhole people, or to compete with them. We're here to see, to share, to learn, to understand, to grow, to celebrate, to cherish. Life isn't about surviving, it's about thriving. And a lot of the time, we get in our own way and become our own obstacles. Drop the stance, remove the blinders, try not to cling to a picture in your head of how things should be or how people should be. Don't be so sure that you already know what someone will say. Do not assume you've gathered all there is to know about your partner, even if, and especially if, you've been together for years. Try not to make snap judgements about people based on one conversation, one interaction, no matter how wonderful or miserable. Get in the water and swim and observe all the animals having lives of their own.

Speak Out

Clear communication is so important, but it's not always easy. Sometimes people don't say what they feel out of fear that the truth will hurt. Sometimes people are afraid to say what's in their hearts because it means that change is inevitable. And of course, when you're sharing something with someone, you always want to express yourself with compassion. So many people seem to struggle when it comes to speaking out about what is true for them, in big ways and small.

First of all, in-person communication is always the best bet when you're saying something that's emotional, sensitive in nature, or has a "charge" to it. Understand that so much can get lost in translation with emails and texts. If you can't meet face-to-face, a phone call is your next best bet; at least you can hear the person's voice. You can hear the tone, or their voice cracking, or a sigh or sniffle. You can hear the frustration, and the pain underneath it. Words on a screen are impersonal. People get reckless with their fingertips. They write things they'd never say. A text is not a place to break up with someone, and neither is an email. If you're frustrated or angry, go ahead and write it down if you need to get clear about the storm that's raging in your mind, but don't hit "send" until you're in a calm state of mind. Words are powerful. Once you put them out there, you can't take them back. And some things are so hurtful, they may be forgiven, but it's unlikely they'll be forgotten.

Manipulation is no way to go about getting what you want. If you want something, or you need something, say it. You may not get it, but take the mystery and agony out of things for yourself, and the people in your life. No one can read your mind, or mine. Being passive aggressive is also not a fabulous communication style. Expecting people to try to figure out what's wrong or what you need makes it harder on everyone. If you're angry, disappointed, scared, sad, hurt or confused, try saying that out loud.

When we're angry, it's almost always just a cover for our hurt feelings. If we're defensive, it's because we feel attacked, even if that's just our perception. Many people cannot receive anything but positive feedback. If you offer any kind of constructive input, that, too, might be received as an attack. Sometimes this happens with personality disorders like narcissism. Sometimes it happens because a person grew up in an abusive household, and an admission of error was met with intense pain and punishment. You really don't know what someone is dealing with unless they tell you. But you can work on the way you express yourself. You can work toward clear, truthful, compassionate communication. That's really all you can do. As with everything, you can never control what someone else does.

Sometimes we keep quiet because we don't want to have uncomfortable conversations, or we think we already know what the other person will say. And let me say this. If you have a long history with someone, and you know that sane, satisfying communication isn't possible, then don't bark up that tree. Accept people where they are and how they are, or don't have them in your life, or have them in your life, but create boundaries. In general, though, if you struggle with being assertive, work on it. Most people will really appreciate your honesty, if you're kind. Being truthful and mean is crappy. It's not funny or brave or strong or tough. It's crappy. So there's that.

If you struggle to say what's real for you, get some help with it. Maybe you grew up and no one ever asked you how you felt, or what you needed or wanted. Perhaps you're still trying to figure that out. Maybe it doesn't occur to you that how you feel is important and worth sharing. Maybe you feel invisible, or believe your worth lies in what you can do for other people. Those are all lies. Find your truth, and then find your voice. It really matters.

Grab Your Suit, and Let's Do This

I think a lot of people search for happiness, but a long time ago I started searching for the truth. When I say the truth, I just mean the truth as it exists in my own life; I'm not suggesting what's true for me is true for you. I just don't believe it's possible to find any kind of inner peace if you're lying to yourself in any way, or refusing to accept the reality about relationships or situations in your life. That means knowing yourself, understanding what lights you up, recognizing when you don't show up the way you'd like to and examining what happened for you so you can do it differently the next time. Being accountable for the energy you're spreading, being aware of the things you're feeling and saying and doing. That kind of truth.

Blaming other people for your unhappiness (which I certainly used to do), is a form of lying to yourself. If you're over 25 (and I'd really kind of like to say 20), and you are not happy with the way your life looks and feels, it is on you, now. No matter what may be behind you, what you've gone through, or how many different ways you've been hurt or disappointed, only you are responsible for your own happiness.

Clinging, manipulating and numbing out are all forms of lying to yourself. Love is not something you force. It's something you give, freely, with the understanding that you may be hurt. Sometimes you'll get hurt because we are always growing, and two people don't always grow together. Sometimes you'll be hurt as a result of where a person is on his or her particular path. People can only be where they are, they can only give what they've got. If you don't accept the truth of the situation, you are in for a world of pain.

We all know when things just don't "feel right." There's no hiding from that reality, but people try to do that all the time. They hide with busy-ness or distraction or drinking until they're comfortably numb. With shopping or decorating or eating or not eating or video games. With trying to manage another person's journey, or trying to cajole the love out of them. Love is not a sales pitch. You should not have to prove you're worthy of it. If you feel you do, you need to stop everything and figure out how you could not know that you are, because that is some deep pain. That is the number one thing you'd better get busy healing. And time passes in the fog of a lie. It won't get you anywhere. Wherever you go, you will bring the pain of the lie with you, and you will have to use most of your energy to push it down. You will make yourself sick in your soul.

I would rather know the truth and be in pain than sleepwalk in a lie. There is no beauty in delusion. The truth to me is a comfort, even if it cuts down the center of my heart. Because it's real and I know I'm awake. I don't want to distract myself from life, I want to be soaked in it. I want to swim, you know? I do not expect smooth waters all the time. We are all going to be thrown against the rocks in life. In my experience, that's when the growth happens. When you're cut and bleeding and you think, "How did I not see this coming? Why did I swim this way, and hang out here in the storm for so long? Why don't I love myself?" You need to find the answers to those questions if this is speaking to you. And you know, sometimes you love yourself but a storm hits, anyway.

This may sound kind of dark, but it isn't at all. It's simply that life is full of joy and pain, of darkness and light, of laughter that comes from your very center, and tears that come from that same place, too. And if you're awake and swimming, you will also be there to appreciate and soak in all the love, all the joy, all the yes of life. The incredible moments when someone looks you in the eye and you know you are being seen. Understood. Celebrated.

You'll know that that's real, too. If you want to be happy, you're going to have to swim in the ocean of your truth. That's where the love is. That's where you find your happy. Grab your suit and start paddling.

CHAPTER 5: COMPARING AND CONTRASTING DISEASE

Do you ever have a day when you're feeling down, and you get on social media and feel even worse, because it seems that everyone else is having this perfect life with their perfect job, house, car, dog, handstand, vacation...fill-in-the-blank? Few things make us feel more alienated than comparing and contrasting our experience with someone else's, but it's what we're trained to do. "Keeping up with the Jones'" is a way of life, but it's also a sickness. No one else is going to take your place in the sun. You have something to offer no one else can, and you have to trust in that. There's no formula for life, there's just your own personal process.

There's also the common practice of creating an "us versus them" point of view. We love to categorize. We love what's familiar to us, and tend to fear the unknown, but the more we look for the similarities, the more we feed empathy and compassion. And that comes in handy on those days when we're feeling "less than." How it is within us is how it is around us.

Love More, Judge Less

On Tuesday mornings I volunteer for an hour in my daughter's Kindergarten class. It's extremely fun. I love my daughter's teacher. She's very warm, but very firm, and she maintains standards in the room. The kids have to listen to each other. They have to keep their hands to themselves. They don't have to agree with each other, but they have to be respectful. She's really setting them up with great tools for life.

Last week when I was there, one of the little girls was sitting at my table, and she crossed herself when an ambulance went by, and said something under her breath. I knew what she was doing, but she looked up at me with this little smile, and said, "I'm praying that everyone is okay." She's five. I told her that I do that, too, but I don't use my hands. One of the other kids asked what she was doing with her hands, and she explained that she was asking God to take care of anyone who might be hurt. One of the kids asked what "God" was. I said it was a word that meant different things to different people, and that was a topic she could explore with her mom or dad. And we had a conversation about what it means to care about people, whether we know them or not. It was easily the best conversation of my week.

We get so caught up with labels and separation. We try to figure out who's like us, and who's different. We're so prone to create an us and a them. But true spirituality doesn't discriminate. It doesn't separate. It asks us to care about everyone, because we're all part of the same family. I know it's not easy, but if we start to expand that same idea to all living creatures, and the planet itself, we start to shift the way we've been moving through the world. Sometimes we learn things at home, like hatred. Hatred can be passed down from generation to generation, just like eye-color. When we're little, our parents are god-like creatures, and it doesn't occur to us to challenge what we're being taught or told until we get old enough to realize we're our own being. We have our own mind and our own heart and our own ability to discern and intuit and make sense of the world.

Hatred is a great divider, and it weakens its host. When we hate, we're blind. In my opinion, it's also unnatural to us. I spend a lot of time with little kids, not just because I have two of my own. I always have, because my little brother is eleven years younger than me. I've had a little person trailing around after me asking why questions for most of my life. We come into this world full of love and curiosity. We're trusting and open, unless or until we have a reason not to be. Kids might ask guileless questions, like why someone has a different skin color, or why they observe different holidays, but it's never with contempt. It's with a genuine desire to understand. And kids do what we do, not what we say, as we well know.

Maybe you don't have kids, and maybe you don't want them. But you were a child once, and it's good to examine your beliefs about yourself, about other people, and about the world around you. Sometimes something we've learned is so ingrained, we don't even question it. I get emails from people who were told they were mistakes. That they'd never amount to anything. That they were meant to be seen and not heard. That their parents wanted a boy, not a girl. That they're a disappointment.

Also, you can preach compassion all day long, but if you're hard on yourself, don't think that will go unnoticed by your kids. We internalize everything. We're energetic creatures, and we both emit and absorb energy wherever we go. If your mother was always dieting and scrunching up her face when she looked at herself in the mirror, even if she always told you you were beautiful, don't be surprised if you have body-image issues. If you were taught that people who didn't believe the same things your family believed were wrong or not to be trusted, you're going to have some unlearning to do.

The outside might look different. And I mean this for all of us. We may be male or female, short or tall, thin or stocky, dark or light. We may believe in one god, many gods, or no god at all. We may believe in a continuation of consciousness, or we may believe in the great nothing when it all ends. We may be rich, or we may struggle to put food on the table. The bottom line is that we all deal with certain parameters. We have a finite amount of time in the body we're in. We have the capacity to love people wildly, openly, with everything we've got. We have our attachments, our fears, our dreams, our heartbreaks, our nights when we cry ourselves to sleep, or wonder what we're doing here, or flail about trying to find our place in the world. The more we look for the vulnerability behind the mask, the kid underneath the grown-up, the similarities instead of the differences, the kinder we become. And the world could really use that right about now.

Yes, there are some people who've closed their hearts and fed their hatred, and are so far off the grid, there's not much hope for any kind of epiphany at this point, but that's a tiny percentage of human beings on planet earth. The vast majority of people recognize that an us versus them mentality isn't getting the job done. It isn't creating a world that's safe for us, or for our children. And it also doesn't have to be this way. Examine your thoughts, your words and your actions. Maybe you're already operating from a place of love most of the time, but maybe you're still struggling with this. Start with your own internal dialogue. Since there's no (good) escape from the voice inside your head, begin to starve a loud inner critic if you have one.

You don't have to believe everything you think. Sometimes our thoughts about ourselves are so violent, so unforgiving, so relentless, it's a wonder we can get out of bed in the morning. And if you're that hard on yourself, I guarantee you're hard on other people, too. Perhaps not as harsh as you are with yourself, but whatever we have within us is what we spread. Start there. It might seem like a small thing, but if everyone worked on creating a peaceful and loving world within themselves, the whole landscape around us would change. If you're in the habit of saying things like, "I'm such an idiot!" when you make a mistake, shift that thought to something like, "I'm human and I make mistakes sometimes, and that's okay, and very normal. Let me take a deep breath and see what I can do." Find a nickname for yourself that makes you smile, like, "Chief", or, "Sport", or "Tiger", and whenever you feel that self-loathing come up, catch yourself, with an, "Okay, Sport, that didn't go the way we wanted it to, but it's no big deal." What I'm trying to say is that you really want an inner voice that roots you on, not one that tears you down. May we all send good thoughts and love when we hear an ambulance go by. May we all care about each other more, and judge each other less. May all beings be free from suffering. May all beings be happy.

Be a Survivor, Not a Victim

One of the worst things you can feed is a victim mentality. And let's get right to it—sometimes horrendous, heartbreaking things happen to kind and beautiful people. Maybe you grew up in an unsafe environment and spent most of your childhood trying to be invisible or indispensable. Maybe you saw things and experienced things no one ever should. Maybe you grew up and had a terrifying interaction that turned everything you thought you knew inside out. And maybe you've endured a loss that feels impossible to comprehend. These things are all possible. I hope none of them have happened to you, but they're all possible.

I say this to you with total compassion and empathy. I really, truly get that life can break your heart sometimes, but it will never, ever serve you to define yourself as a victim. Your much better option is to choose the role of survivor. Life is not fair. We all want to make it make sense, we want to create order out of chaos and uncertainty, but it can't be done.

The pain in this life is real, and it's not dosed out in equal amounts. So if you're reading this and you've had to carry something that hurts so much it's hard to breathe, I get it. And of course there are less dramatic events that might cause a person to feel that life isn't fair, and that they have a rotten hand to play. Again and again, it comes down to what you're going to feed. Of course if you've suffered losses you have to give yourself time and space to mourn and grieve. And how much time and how much space is completely personal, and something only you can move through.

I'm not talking about grieving, though. I'm talking about letting your losses and experiences harden you, so you're moving through the world bitterly. When we tell ourselves that things have happened that have broken us, for example, when we define ourselves as broken, the implication is that we cannot be healed. When we clutch a story to our chest that explains and excuses why we are the way we are, we're also letting ourselves off the hook for doing anything about it. You can't control what's happened, but you can certainly decide how you're going to respond.

I see so many people who cling to their rage like a shield. Who dig their heels in and demand that everyone acknowledge their version of reality. Who recite their list of ways they've been wronged. The thing is, it's exhausting. It's like a full-time job to be that enraged. You really can't get much else done. And it's such a miserable state to be in, of course you want to numb out and check out, and look to external things or people to make it better. It's not like bitterness feels good.

Whatever has happened might shape you, but it doesn't have to rule you. At a certain point, at any point, you can decide to take ownership of your life. You can figure out what you might be able to change, and get to work changing it. This might be the way you interact with people, it may be the tone and message of your inner voice that needs work. Some things you won't be able to change. Other people would fall into that category. You can never change what someone else needs or wants or says or does, but you can always change the way you respond. You can decide to rise up; with every breath, there's the potential to begin again. If we're pitying ourselves, we're stuck in the past. We're dragging the past along with us into our present, and holding it up for everyone to see, even our brand-new friends, and we're demanding that other people reckon with our past, when that job is ours. If they want us, they have to accept this whole bunch of baggage, too. But they don't. And we don't have to drag it along with us, either.

A pity party isn't very fun; you'll probably have a tough time getting people to show up. But someone who looks their pain in the face and then deals with it (whether that means reaching out for support, or exploring healing modalities until they find something that works for them), that's a person who's ready to live. If you want to be free of your pain, you have to reckon with it. You don't bow down and let it own you, you challenge it to a duel on a bright day, so you can bring all that darkness into the light and take a look at what you're facing.

The Green-Eyed Monster

Let's crack open the green-eyed monster. I'm talking about envy, but while we're at it, let's tackle jealousy, doubt, insecurity, fear, a history of betrayal, doubt about self-worth, and abandonment issues, too, shall we?

When we envy what someone else has, it's because we're coming from a place of lack. We've stopped focusing on all that we do have, and have become transfixed and obsessed with what we don't have. When we're envious, we fear that someone else has taken up our space in the sun. Now our chance is gone, because the sun can only shine on that other person. And any hopes we'd had are dashed, and we never get any breaks, anyway, and maybe we just have really bad karma. Or maybe that other person is a lying, cheating whore who'll stop at nothing to get what s/he wants. You see what I'm saying? The green-eyed monster isn't at all pretty. And it has bitter breath, too. It gets in our heads and tells us tales of how we don't measure up and probably never will. And you can choose to feed the monster with your fear, or you can send it packing. But I'll get back to that.

Jealousy is a close cousin of envy. We worry that someone else may have something we don't, or may take something we have. We doubt our own value. We feel threatened and insecure, and we focus on our perceived weaknesses. We dwell on what could happen, we worry about imagined slights. Jealousy makes us sick, and if we let the sickness grow, the symptoms are ugly. Jealousy makes a person check their partner's texts, emails, pockets. Jealousy whispers that what you treasure most could be stolen from you. You can feed that fear, or you can send jealousy packing, too. But I'll get back to that.

You may have a history of having been disappointed, disrespected, betrayed, unheard or unseen. Maybe you put up with treatment you never thought you would. Maybe you were left as a child, or maybe it happened later, at the hands of the first person with whom you really, truly fell in love. Maybe you think everyone cheats, simply because everyone you've picked has cheated. Maybe you're so worried about being left or betrayed, you bend over backwards to be perfect so that there's no way your current partner would do those things to you, but they don't get to really know you, either. And you know that they don't, so the relationship won't be satisfying, anyway. You'll be "perfect" for them, and unfulfilled. Unseen, unknown.

When we doubt our worth, it's because some deep part of us thinks we might not be truly lovable. There's something in us that believes we might be easy to leave, or betray, or disrespect. Let me circle back, here. How do you send envy, jealousy, doubt and fear, packing? You pick up your mind and direct it toward all the things you do have. You remind yourself that this particular group of cells that make up the person you call you, has never come together before, and will never come together this way again. You remind yourself that you have your health, you have people in your life you love beyond words. You have people in your life who know you and see you and cherish you. You have a particular, gorgeous song to sing. You have a beautiful, tender heart. And you have gifts only you can share. If you start to train your mind on all that abundance, the nasty green-eyed monster will climb out of your head and slide off your chest and vaporize before you so you can breathe again.

Be mindful about what you're feeding yourself. When you're feeling vulnerable and insecure, try not to push those feelings away. See if you can lean into them, and find the source of your doubt and fear. What's really bothering you? What's happening now, and is it reminiscent of something that happened long ago, that pierced you and made you doubt your own beauty?

If you find yourself trolling around on social media, feeling sick because everyone's statuses are pithy and positive, everyone's pictures are shiny and insta-perfect, and you feel like crawling in a hole with a bag over your head, try to breathe. We all have those days. Everyone you encounter has pain. Most people don't put that stuff in their updates.

You are not here to worry that you aren't good enough. You are not here to chase after people who don't see you. You are not here to convince anyone else of your own worth. You are not here to be in relationships with people who make you feel sick and full of fear, wondering if you're going crazy, or if it's them. You really aren't. Life is too short for all of that. If you're not sure you're lovable, you'll save yourself a lot of time, energy and heartache if you deal with that doubt before you try to do anything else, like be in a relationship, or follow your dreams. Those things are hard enough to do when we feel good about ourselves. It's near-impossible when you're riddled with self-loathing and anxiety. Wishing you love, peace, strength, and the ability to focus on everything that is right and good about you. There's a lot.

ALLY HAMILTON

Please Do Not Feed the Fears

Unless we're talking about the good kind of fear that stops you from being reckless with yourself, or makes the hairs on the back of your neck stand up because you're in danger, fear is nothing more than a bully. I'm talking about the kind of fear that stops you from doing what you know in your heart you must. The kind of fear that tells you you're not good enough, you don't have what it takes, you can't do it. That kind of fear can kiss my ass, and it should kiss yours, too.

Fear puts the mind and the heart in a grip. It shuts down our vision so we can only see what isn't going well, what could go wrong, all the reasons why we're stuck. Fear travels with doubt and resentment and envy, with a healthy side of criticism. Fear is not kind, and neither are people living in fear, because fear puts you on the defensive. Sometimes when we don't get what we hope for, we become afraid. "I had a vision of how this thing was supposed to go, how I wanted it to go, and now what do I do?" And the mind starts racing with how awful everything is, how nothing is going right, how things are easier for other people (because fear feeds that comparing and contrasting mind). If you want to shut yourself down and close yourself up and do life in such a way that you're always wearing blinders and feeding yourself can't, then fear is the way to go. But, seriously, who wants to live like that? Shut down and numbed out and hopeless and frustrated? Alone and angry and confused, waiting for that magical time when "things will get better"?

Things are not going to get better unless you open to love. And you cannot do that if you are wrapped in a tight little ball with your fists clenched and your eyes scrunched up, and your head full of shouldn't. Or stories about why you can't, why you're incapable of change, or so numb you really can't feel anything. So addicted to distraction the weeks fly by, then the months, then the years, and oh crap, now it's too late. Anyone who is not suffering from afflictions beyond their control can heal. I'm going to say that again. Everyone. Can. Heal. Love requires courage, participation, and ownership of your own experience.

Love is not for those who won't be vulnerable, because when you open your heart, there's always the possibility you're going to get hurt. But you know what? I'd rather have my heart broken fully, deeply, right through the center than live my life asleep and curled up in a ball in a corner wondering what, exactly, I'm doing here. I'd rather be awake with my heart open wide and my head full of Yes, than numbing myself out to avoid my pain. The pain is the path to healing. The pain is where you head. You walk straight into the center of it, and you do not come out until you have faced that sh&t down. Or it owns you. Those are your choices, there is no third, "Can it be a little easier because I don't want to work that hard?" option.

I refuse to allow any person or any circumstance to rob me of my purpose here, and I hope you do, too. Because anything else is a pure waste of your time, and you aren't given enough to waste. This is your beautiful, complicated, confusing, joyous, sometimes deeply lonely, other times amazingly incredible life, where sometimes you have your heart broken, and sometimes you feel it expand so much you think it's going to come right out of your chest. "This love is so much, so full, so deep it's going to carry me up above the trees, and over the ocean, and oh, wait, it IS the ocean." Why, why, why would you deny yourself love like that? Because of some fear? Totally not acceptable. I hope you got a taste of the love I'm sending your way. It has a side of ass-kick, I know. But sometimes that's the kind of love we need. If you just need a hug right now, I'm down for that, too.

CHAPTER 6: DON'T CHASE LOVE

So many people suffer from the delusion that they aren't worthy of love, it would blow your mind. So if you're in that camp, don't despair, because you're certainly not alone. However, there's another, wonderful camp where people actually have fun, and it's called Love Camp. Anyone can join, and the activities are limitless. You get to design your own curriculum. But you have to turn in your membership card to that other camp, first.

Direct Your Energy

Not everyone is going to like you, or me. That's just a reality of life. Sometimes we'll be misunderstood, judged, rejected, excluded, or ignored. None of these things feel good, but human beings are complex. Some people need to be angry, or they need for you to be the bad guy, or they need to rewrite history so they can live with themselves. There's nothing you can do about that. If a person won't or can't communicate in a respectful and compassionate way, there isn't a lot of hope for mutual understanding or closure. On the flip side, sometimes we'll screw up, and we may not be met with forgiveness. Once you've owned your mistakes and apologized, there's not much more you can do.

Sometimes we spend our energy on the people who are looking to bring us down, thereby using up energy we could have spent on the people who can see us clearly. And look, I'm not saying we're all wonderful. We all have work to do, places to heal, ways we could show up for ourselves and the people in our lives that might be infused with more enthusiasm or presence or gratitude. But I'm talking about the tendency to get snagged on those people who are full of venom. Sometimes you're dealing with a personality disorder, but if you try to rationalize with someone who cannot hear reason, you're as nuts as they are. It's not like we have all the time in the world. And where and how you direct your energy has the biggest impact on how your life will feel.

By the same token, sometimes we dwell on all the things we don't have, and all the ways life is presenting its challenges, when we could be focusing on those things that are flowing, and are fulfilling. I'm not saying we should shun people who are struggling, in pain, or full of rage. Compassion is always the path. But to spend hours, days, weeks, years getting caught up in other people's dramas is not the best use of your time.

You have a song to sing. You have dreams, fears, things that inspire you, and excite you. You probably have a vision of how you'd like life to be or to feel, gifts within you that you long to share, ideas that you'd love to see blossom into being. That's where you want to direct your energy. There will always be barking dogs, or, in the vernacular of our time, "haters gonna hate." Don't allow too much of your precious time and energy to go toward that stuff, and try not to dwell on what you're lacking at this particular point in time.

It's not always a choice, but the more we can choose to be grateful for all we have, the better we're going to feel. This is not realistic when you're dealing with heartache, rage, grief, jealousy, guilt or shame. I'm not one of those, "It's always in your power to be happy in every moment" kind of yogis. Real, actual, devastating things happen sometimes, and your best bet is to feel all of your feelings. We don't take the road marked, "Spiritual Bypass" here. But short of tragedies and great losses, direct your energy toward the good stuff. You're not going to get to the end of your life and think, "I wish I'd been angry and defensive more. I wish I'd held onto my righteousness a little more fervently. Too bad I didn't judge and gossip more of the time."

Go rock your life. Open your heart. Nurture yourself and the people close to you. Care about everyone, but don't get stuck in a ditch with people who do nothing but hurt you. You aren't here for that.

A Bridge Takes Two

If you have a long history with someone, and you have healing to do around your relationship or events of the past, understand you can never do one hundred percent of the work alone. I'm talking about important long-term relationships in your life, with family members, or spouses, or your best friend for years and years. Life is not easy. It's amazing and interesting. It's filled with incredible beauty, the potential for love so intense you feel your heart might burst, and pain that can bring you to your knees. It's always changing, so it's certainly an adventure. But there's a tremendous amount of uncertainty, and not everyone is able to handle that easily. Sometimes people cling to their pain or their anger because that feels safer than letting go. And the reality is, the people in the most pain are also the people who create the most pain. It's not usually intentional. What we have within us is what we spread around us.

If you've been disappointed, neglected, abused or abandoned, those are all experiences which might have hardened you, or broken your trust in people. I understand that. But I think it's important to believe in the goodness of people, and to understand when you've been betrayed or abandoned by someone, it's not a reflection on you, or your worthiness or ability to receive love, it's a reflection of where the other party is on his or her own path. That doesn't mean it's okay if someone abuses you or mistreats you, it just makes it easier not to take those things personally. I think the key is to be discerning. And to understand that it takes a long time to know a person. We all want love and connection, but your heart is precious and it's important not to be reckless with it. There's a big difference between living in fear, which is not really living, and taking your time.

The thing is, human beings are complicated. We all have our histories, our pain, our various upbringings, ways we were nurtured, loved, supported, or not so much. So when you bring any two people together, it's exponentially more complex. And when you increase that number to three or four or five (as in, a family), you can bet the chances for different dynamics to arise just multiplies. I get emails from so many people in pain over their strained or nonexistent relationships with their mothers or fathers, sons or daughters, sisters or brothers, friends from childhood. Things happen in life. Sometimes a person is moving through pain and they lash out. Or there's a family system in place and roles are being played and maybe it's not a healthy scene, and then one day, one of the players doesn't like his or her role anymore, and everyone panics as the system collapses. Or the whole family is held hostage by one member's addiction, depression, or mental illness. There's no shortage of different scenarios. People fight over money (it isn't usually really the money they're fighting about), or something someone said at a wedding when they were drunk and full of salmon.

But if you have healing to do with someone, understand you need some kind of bridge. It takes two to tango, and it takes two to mend a bridge that has collapsed. I don't think a person has to meet you halfway. It's ideal, but not everyone will be up to that. A person has to step onto the bridge. If you feel motivated to walk the rest of the way, that's enough. But if a person won't even take that first step, you'll be dealing with a chasm. And it will be up to you how you want to manage that. Sometimes we can't have a person in our lives. And sometimes we have to accept that a relationship will never be quite what we want it to be. Not everyone is up to fearless and honest communication and acceptance. Not everyone can open his or her mind to a different point of view. You can't force someone to be somewhere they aren't.

Sometimes we have to choose between two painful options. Not having someone in our lives, or having them in our lives in a way that falls incredibly short of what we know is possible. That's a choice only you can make. You can keep your hands open. You can offer the chance for healing. But you can't make someone take you up on it, and I know that can hurt. I think closing yourself down and shutting yourself off hurts more, though.

What You Allow

You can't control what other people will do or say, but you can choose the way you'll respond. This comes up in so many areas. Maybe you have a family member who has a history of being verbally and emotionally abusive, and now you've gotten to the point where you simply don't want to subject yourself to that treatment any longer. Lots of things can get us to that place. We're always evolving. Maybe you've reached a point in your healing process where you're ready to set boundaries. Maybe you have children now, and you're able to speak up on their behalf, even though you've never been able to stand up for yourself.

Whatever it is, you won't change the offending party. But you can definitely change the way you interact with him or her. Speaking calmly, but with confidence about your experience is a gift you give yourself, and everyone in your life. Being able to say, "When you do this, it makes me feel X, and X is not okay for me anymore. So from now on, when I come to town for a visit, I'll stay at a hotel. We'll see how things go. If you're unable to not do or say X, then at least I can remove myself from the situation." You're taking responsibility for your feelings. You're not blaming them or making them wrong, you're just stating how things are for you, and how you'll be honoring what's true for you. If the other party tells you not to come if that's how it's going to be, so be it. You aren't here to be a punching bag for anyone. If the requirement is for you to subject yourself to behavior or comments that are hurtful, that's too great a cost. If a person can't be kind and loving, if that's too much to ask, they don't belong in your life. If you want them in your life anyway, then you have to set boundaries that work for you. And if even those can't be respected, then you're left with no choice but to walk away.

When we start to make changes in the way we relate to the people around us, you can bet there's going to be push-back. This is especially true if we're shifting a role we've always played. I used to be a lot less assertive. Sometimes people would say hurtful or inappropriate things to me, and I'd collapse in on myself and internalize the experience. I'd have the feeling of being punched in the stomach, way down where it really hurts. But no words would come out of my mouth. When that started shifting for me, I was met with resistance and threats and rage. How dare I stand up for myself? But that's your job, that's your work. You carve out a place for yourself and a way of being that brings you peace and joy. And you don't sacrifice that for anyone. Most people come around. They might scream and yell and wave their arms, but eventually, most people will quiet down and shift the way they deal with you. So you're not changing them or teaching them or making them wrong, you're just requiring a certain level of respect and consideration. You're changing the rules of engagement.

This is an essential component of healing. You have to be able to act on your own behalf. You have to value your own tender heart, and your peace of mind, and your ability to look yourself in the mirror at the end of the day when you're brushing your teeth. When we allow ourselves to be mistreated, we also betray ourselves. And it's hard to face that. If you grew up feeling powerless, it's likely that you regress to that stance when you feel confronted. And when you start trying to assert yourself, it will probably come out with more force than you intend. And that's okay. You can tell the people in your life that you're trying to change some profound things about the way you're moving through the world, because the way you've been doing it so far is not working for you. You can explain that you're working on standing up for yourself, and speaking up when things don't feel good or right, but that this is a new experience, and you're still birthing into this new way of being, and it isn't all going to be pretty. Maybe they'll take that in, and maybe they won't. You're not responsible for managing anyone else's reactions or path, you're just responsible for your own clear communication. Practice with people you trust. Like anything else, the more you do it, the easier it gets.

Moving through life allowing yourself to be disrespected by the people closest to you, or by complete strangers, is not going to work. It's too much to bear.

Free Yourself

Sometimes you realize you're being held hostage by someone else's instability, mental illness, or addiction. This can only happen if you care deeply in the first place; that is, if you're invested in the relationship, or if this person is in your life and it's not easy to extricate yourself from all communication or connection (your boss or colleague, for example).

Often, we meet people and they may present one face to us, but inside it's a whole different story. It takes time to get to know people, and even time won't get the job done if a person wants to keep things from you. We only ever know the interior world of another person if they give us access to it.

If you're a warm, trusting, open person, you probably project and assume that other people are also that way. That's what we all tend to do, we make assumptions about other people based on how things are for us. And that's a great way to have your eyes opened, but it probably won't feel very good. Because we can never assume, and we can never project. We all have our various upbringings, experiences, ways we were supported or neglected, different tendencies and dreams, varied emotional lives, relationships, things that are driving us consciously or unconsciously, heartbreaks, levels of resiliency, disappointments, achievements and fears. How things are for me is not how they are for you, but we exist in this same world. We just cannot expect other people to see what we see, even the things that seem totally obvious to us.

People with addictive personalities are usually very good at hiding their addictions or tendencies. And I don't say that without compassion. It's awful to be a slave to a numbing agent. To feel like you have to have access to your "fix" at all times, whether we're talking about drugs and alcohol, or sex, or the internet, or shopping, or eating disorders. So you might observe erratic behavior in someone you're getting to know, but think it's just an "off day" here and there.

Mental illness can work the same way. Maybe you're dealing with a personality disorder that renders a person unable to consider how their actions impact the people around them, but unless you're a target, you might go a good long while before feeling like something isn't right.

Sometimes, in order to be close to someone, you have to accept their version of reality. Maybe you've known people like this. I once had a girlfriend who had a serious drinking problem. When I'd try to talk to her about it, she'd say she was a social drinker, and I was overworrying. But I poured her into a cab enough times to know this wasn't something to sweep under the rug. I talked to her mother about it, but she wasn't ready to face it, either. And when I refused to be quiet about it, my friend wrote me off. In certain situations, there's nothing you can do but walk away and hope a person decides to get help before it's too late.

There are many people attached to their stories about what's happened in their past, and why things are the way they are, and why they are the way they are. I lived that way during my late teens and early twenties, and it was awful. Blame keeps you stuck pointing, when you really want to be digging. You'll find most people living this way are angry or bitter or depressed, and probably all three. I once became friends with a guy who had story after story about how he'd been screwed professionally. First by this company, then by another. And I believed him, I believed he'd been unfairly overlooked, unappreciated, and mistreated. But then he went to work for close friends of mine, and I watched him blatantly sabotage every opportunity he had to grow. He was more attached to the sad story than he was to writing a new one. When I tried to point that out to him, he became enraged. Sometimes people cling to their stories because they aren't ready to take ownership of their lives yet. They use their anger like a shield, and anything you try to say or do bounces off. It's understandable. We all have our coping mechanisms, and you can't make a person be somewhere they are not.

If you're attracted to the "walking wounded", you're probably going to encounter people like this. And I'll just remind you in case you need to be reminded, you cannot save anyone. You can love people and you can try to get them help and support, but you can't make another person happy, or compassionate or kind or loving. You can't make anyone fall in love with you. You're not going to change the way someone moves through the world. This is all inside work; everyone has to do their own journey. You can decide who you want to bring close, and who you want to keep at a distance. Often, you won't have to make these decisions, they'll be made for you. If you back someone against the wall and ask them to be accountable for what they've done, and they aren't ready to do that, they'll head for the hills, anyway. But pay attention to your tendency to draw people in, who aren't able to do anything but hurt you. Don't participate in someone else's instability. You can't fix it, but it also doesn't help when you enable it. It doesn't help them, and it doesn't help you. Create boundaries where necessary, and defend them when you must. You can't control what other people do or say or feel or want or need, but you can control the way you choose to respond. Just keep your own side of the street clean, the rest will take care of itself.

Don't Chase Love

Whenever you find yourself trying to force or control an outcome, it's time to perk up and take a look at what's happening within you. We're all going to be attached to certain ideas; this is the nature of being human. For example, we'll all want our loved ones to be happy. Perfectly understandable. But if we start to assume that we know what will make someone else happy, then we're in trouble. The minute you try to manage someone else's path, you're losing a chance to manage your own.

A lot of the time, we're taking things personally. Maybe there's someone we really care for, and we're chasing. Right there, it's a problem. You don't chase love, you open to it. If you have to take off after it, that's a huge red flag. Instead of spending your time and energy wondering what you can do to be perfect for this other person so you can get their attention and make them fall in love with you, you could be examining why you're feeling so badly about yourself you'd tie up your Nike's and chase your worthiness. You're worthy. You're the only one of you we get.

You think you aren't worthy of love? If someone isn't offering it to you fully and openly, what are you doing?

Have you ever talked to a couple who's in love, and has been for thirty, forty, fifty years? I have. I make a habit of it any chance I get. I love to see couples who make it. And not once, in all the conversations with all the people I've met over the years, has any couple told me a story about a beginning that involved one person feeling deeply insecure all the time, and the other not treating them well. That's not a solid foundation, and it won't lead anywhere good. Also, it isn't loving to race after someone who doesn't want to be caught. If you love someone, you have to want for them what they want for themselves. If someone is making it clear to you that they aren't available the way you want them to be, it's disrespectful to refuse to accept that. It's not just disrespectful to them and their feelings, it's disrespecting yourself to keep trying.

It can hurt like hell when people we love don't want what we wish they would want. This happens when we relate to the world and the people around us as if it's about us. As if we're in the center of this thing, and everything is happening to us. When you can remove yourself from the center of the story and look at it from the sidelines, you'll see it usually has very little to do with you. People want what they want. They are where they are. They have the tools they have. They may not want you, or anyone else, the way you wish that they would. But it's also a bit nuts of us to imagine we can ever know what's right for someone else. Isn't it hard enough to grapple with what you need for your own inner peace? As long as a person isn't intentionally hurting you or anyone else, you really have to assume they're doing the best they can to work life out in a way that will feel good to them. Sometimes people don't know what they want, and that can be hard to watch and hard to walk away from if you're hoping maybe they'll finally realize they want you. But you aren't here to wait.

When we start to try to control situations or people, when we find ourselves attempting to manipulate or cajole, or dance like a monkey to get what we want, it's time to stop and check ourselves. Life is not about forcing the picture in your head onto the people around you. That picture of "how things should be." No one will thank you for trying. And not many things cause us more pain than our attachment to that picture. It can be so hard to let it go, I really understand that. But grasping and waiting and hoping and struggling and doubting and obsessing….that's no way to live.

It's brutal to have to release an idea, or another person, or a hope we held close. But you can't cling and fly at the same time. And you don't have all the time in the world. So I wouldn't spend too much of it refusing to accept, and open to, things as they are. There's so much power in that. Your self-respect is in the mix. So is your self-esteem. This is the stuff that has far-reaching consequences on your life, on the way you move through the world, and on the way life feels to you, day in, and day out. Let life feel good. It might hurt a lot in the short-term, but intense pain for a little while is so much better than a lifetime of suffering.

Believe Them

A few years ago, I went on a date with a guy who travels around the country giving talks and interviews about compassion and kindness. He's written books, he's been on all kinds of television shows. He's extremely charismatic and funny and smart. We met through mutual friends and he asked me out, and of course, I was very excited. I thought we had a similar outlook on life, and I liked the fact that he seemed down-to-earth.

The night of the date came, and he picked me up, and off we went. The conversation was easy and deep. Definitely no small talk. By the time we were at the restaurant, we were so in the flow, the waiter stopped asking us if we wanted to order. We never made it past a pitcher of mint lemonade. We sat at the table for three hours, drunk on conversation. He made all kinds of references to things we had to do, friends of his I had to meet, places we had to go. There was not an inch of me wondering whether we'd be going out again.

We exchanged a few emails the next day, but he didn't mention plans, and I just assumed he was going to call to do that. So you can imagine, when I hadn't heard from him a week later, I was surprised and confused. I decided to be direct, and sent an email letting him know I'd had a great time. I told him I was really looking forward to getting to know him better. I told him about a public speaking engagement I'd since had, that we'd discussed the night we went out, and how I was pleased I hadn't died from fear, after all. Radio silence. He never wrote back, and I was left with the sting of having made myself vulnerable. I didn't say anything to our mutual friends, because I didn't want them to feel badly, and I also didn't want anyone else to get involved. After numerous conversations with trusted girlfriends, and a couple of close male friends, I let it go. I figured it must have been smoke and mirrors or something. Because it's one thing to talk about kindness and compassion, but it's another thing to have some.

I found out much later he'd been dating someone off and on for a long time. When we went out, they'd been off, but at some point the week after our date, they were on again. I've been in those relationships before. The ones that are so hard to end. The ones where you feel so hooked in you're convinced it must be love so you keep going back, even though you know nothing will be different. Anyway, when I realized what happened, I felt a little soothed, but also angry. It would have been so easy to simply shoot me an email and let me know. It would have been kinder than leaving me to second guess my own experience. To replay the night in my mind and wonder if I'd missed something.

Anyway, who knows why he handled it that way. Probably, he wanted to keep me on the back burner for when his on again went off again. Because I did get an email a few months later, asking if I'd like to have dinner, but by then I was done. I would never pursue something with someone who can't or won't communicate honestly. Most of the time people are not setting out to hurt us. And this was not a major heartbreak, obviously. It was one date. It just so happened it was my first date out of the gate after my divorce, the first date I'd been on in eight years. So the timing wasn't great. But it was a sting, not a wound. Usually people are doing the best they can with the tools they've got. Sometimes people are selfish and prioritize what's good for them over what might be hurtful for someone else. The thing is, it's really never okay to put your discomfort ahead of another person's heart. Awkward conversations aren't fun, but they're so much better than leaving someone in the dark.

The other thing to remember, is that sometimes a person presents themselves one way, but one-on-one, it's a whole different story. This is a guy who does a lot of good, legitimately. But his interpersonal skills need a lot of work. It was a good reminder to me that we should never look at someone's public persona, and assume that's what's happening behind closed doors. Not everybody has every piston firing. And it's easy to take things personally, but most of the time, it's just a reflection of where someone is on their own path; it's not a reflection of anything lacking in you. I get so many emails from people struggling with this stuff. The truth is, if a person is into you, it's not going to be a mystery. You're not going to have to wonder, or chase, or second guess yourself. I really wouldn't waste time with any of that, life is too short, and you are too precious. Save your time and energy for people who are coming at you with everything they've got. And keep your eyes, ears and mind open, so you can see clearly when there's a disconnect between someone's words and their actions. It's really good to remember the Maya Angelou quote, "When people show you who they are, believe them."

CHAPTER 7: ON GRIEF AND HEALING

Loss and vulnerability are natural parts of life, but that doesn't make them easy. Relationships shift and change, we change, too. You are not the you of five years ago, and five years from now, you will not be the you of today. We don't know how long we have here, or what happens after this. And yet, we are asked to show up and love our hearts out.

Sometimes we go through loss that's so large, it's hard to cope. This might be the loss of an entire person, someone we don't know how to live without. It might be the loss of a relationship that's so stitched into the fabric of our existence, we don't know how to create a new canvas. It might be the loss of something that was taken from us, or the loss we experience when we shift away from an old coping mechanism that no longer serves us. Learning to accept that loss is a normal, albeit sometimes devastating part of life here is not easy, but it's part of being at peace. We don't get to choose our experiences all the time, but we suffer more if we refuse to open to them. The idea is to try to grow beauty out of our pain.

Choose the Lesson

Recently, a close friend of mine was left suddenly and without explanation by her husband of less than a year. They were having the normal struggles of any newly married couple, exacerbated by the fact that neither of them had lived with romantic partners before. Just the normal communication issues, and the push-pull we all go through when we're shifting our perspective from "I" to "we." They'd talked about going to counseling, and about making some other changes, too. He'd expressed a desire to move to another part of the country, and she'd been open to that. Throughout the relationship, right up until the day he took off, their text messages were loving, flirtatious and affectionate, their time together was mostly fun, and she had no reason to imagine he'd bail. But one morning he got up, kissed her goodbye as they left the house to go to their respective jobs, and that was the last time she saw him.

When he didn't show up for dinner, she texted, and he said he was out with friends and that he'd probably crash with one of his buddies. She asked him where he was, but he just said he was out having fun, and he'd see her in the morning. And then he didn't show up in the morning, and she called and got his voicemail. When she texted, he said he'd be home later in the day, and that he was running errands. But it turned out he'd gotten on a plane and flown across the country to his parents. She found out from his friend's wife, when she called to see if he knew what was going on.

She flew across the country to see him and sit down face-to-face, but he refused, and his family told her to go away. He wouldn't even respond to her texts, his mother texted to let her know he did not want to see her. She'd spent three years with him, she'd spent plenty of time with his parents and siblings, and not one of them would meet her for a tea, or even get on the phone. Her family and all her close friends, myself included, told her to come home. When there's no communication, there's also no hope. And when his family also shunned her, we all understood this was their modus operandi.

Two weeks later, he served her with divorce papers, citing irreconcilable differences. And then he proceeded to make demands about all the wedding gifts and furniture he wanted. She told me when she saw the list he sent with the movers, the nine-page list of things he wanted them to collect, it finally sank in. He cared about kitchen knives, but not her heart. He wanted the garbage can, but he didn't want to know if she was okay, or how she was coping. He just didn't care.

And so she was left in the dark, trying to figure out what had happened. Was the whole thing a sham? Had he ever loved her? Was the huge wedding he'd wanted just for show? Had he meant anything he'd said on their wedding day, or any day? She told me she felt like she was in the "Twilight Zone", and that at any moment, Rod Serling would step out from behind a closet door, or from around a corner, and tell her she'd entered another dimension.

But life is like this sometimes. We're going along, and BAM! A bomb goes off in the middle of our lives, and everything we thought we knew is just blown to pieces. Sometimes it happens because we're abandoned, like my friend, and sometimes we lose people because they're ripped from us too soon. Sometimes circumstances create the boom. Maybe we're fired, or our house burns down, or we're facing some other huge turn of events we could never have seen coming.

We'd never wish that on ourselves or anyone else, but it happens. And once you feel all the feelings around the experience—the shock, the grief, the confusion, the rage—you have a chance to begin again. Some things are so brutal, you have to accept you're never going to be the same. Some things will never make sense, some things will never be explained, some things will rip your heart out of your chest and eat it with a fine chianti. So be it.

The question is, what are you going to grow out of those ashes? People and circumstances can hurt you, but they can't defeat you unless you let them. You can't rush through your feelings when you're in turmoil; in fact, I'd say that's the moment to use every bit of the support system you have in place, or to get busy creating one. That's when you figure out who in your life is really going to be there for you. And that's really good information to have, because then you know where to invest your time and energy, and with whom.

All you can ever do, is start where you are. We learn and grow from every experience, but we have to choose the lesson. My friend doesn't want anyone to speak badly of her ex, and she isn't fighting him for stuff or money. As she said to me, "The more he takes, the less he has." How's that for choosing the lesson?

There are confounding things that people do to each other sometimes. I get emails from people going through divorce with children, and one partner is using the kids as pawns against the other. Who do you think pays in that scenario? But again, those kids will grow up one day, and they'll choose the lesson. There's a lot of power in that, so if you're in a situation that's making you feel weak, try looking at it from that perspective. No one can take that away from you. Pick the lessons that strengthen you and open you. We have enough hard, closed people in the world. And when things happen that you don't understand, do your very best to have compassion and recognize there's probably more going on than you know. We can only know another person's interior world to the extent that they let us. Many, many people have pain and they don't know how to work with it so they lash out or they take off. Some people suffer from personality disorders that make them incapable of empathy. Some people have been taught that their feelings are the only ones that matter. Imagine how life must be for them. The more they take, the less they have.

You Can't Control the Tides

Sometimes we're trying to control things. It's understandable. We're on a spinning planet and we each have our unknown expiration dates, as do the people we love. We don't know for sure what happens after this. So it's a gig that makes us all inherently vulnerable, and some people have a very hard time with that.

Most of us suffer great losses at some point or another, because the loss of someone we love is like the loss of a whole, gorgeous universe. Anyway, it's not hard to understand why you might want to put your mat down in the same place when you come to yoga. Or why most of us thrive on some routine, some rhythm, something to count on.

Here are some other realities. We are in control of very little. We don't control what life is going to put in our paths. We don't control other people, nor should we try. We don't control what anyone else is going to do, say, want, need, or feel. All we can work on is the way we respond to what we're given, and there's a lot of power in that. Sometimes people do things that are incomprehensible. I know someone who was just abandoned in a cruel and heartless manner when it would have been just as easy to end things with dignity, and to honor the love that was there. But "just as easy" for whom? For me? For you? I mean, from the outside, I can look at the situation and feel astounded. Why would someone do it like that?! With no communication, respect, tenderness? But for me those things are obvious. And probably for you, too.

That's where we get into so much trouble. We start to project what's clear to us onto other people. Shouldn't this be totally obvious to them? And I'd argue that certain things are indisputable. You should treat people the way you want to be treated. You should treat other people's children the way you want your child to be treated. But people can only have the tools they have, and they can only be where they are on their own journeys.

Some people are so full of fear, they can't imagine trusting and being kind and compassionate, because some part of them feels if they do that, they're going to get screwed. I mean, you can't project your world-view onto anyone else, that's my point. And it's easy to take things personally, especially when an intimate relationship comes to an end, and we're left with no explanation or chance for closure. But honestly, if that's the way your partner operates, then they aren't ready for a real relationship with anyone.

Relationships require a willingness to listen and understand, to communicate and to try; without that, there is no relationship. And someone who lacks those tools doesn't lack them because of anything missing in you. The very best thing any of us can do, is work on inner steadiness. Confidence in ourselves to hold and examine whatever life throws in our paths with strength and grace and breath and curiosity.

If you're going through something incomprehensible right now, try meditating on this: This is how it is right now, let me lean into it. Let me allow myself to feel whatever I need to feel, whether it's rage, or grief or confusion or shock, or all of those things. Let me remember that how it is now, is not how it will always be. Let me understand if I missed something along the way. If I sailed by red flags because I didn't want to accept what I knew in my gut. Let me understand if I often override my intuition, or I just got burned this time. Let me know myself. Let me honor and cherish myself. Let me learn and grow from this pain so I have that much more empathy to share when other people in my life suffer. And let me use the heartbreaks to soften and open, so I'm also ready to receive the love and the joy and the astounding beauty when it shows up.

Life is full of everything. You have to be ready.

There's a Lesson in Everything, But Not Everything is a Lesson

It's always good to learn from our experiences. This is how we grow and open, it's how we develop character and begin to know ourselves. There's a lesson in everything, but not everything is a lesson. And I think that's an important distinction to make if you want to be at peace.

I'm a yoga teacher, and I've been teaching for quite a long time, and I know a lot of yoga teachers. So my Facebook newsfeed is filled with inspirational quotes on a pretty frequent basis, and some of them are great, and some of them make me want to stick toothpicks in my eyeballs like they're deviled eggs on a tray at a cocktail party. Sometimes people will post things like, "There are no bad events, there's just the way we respond to them." Oh. Really? There are no bad events? Can anyone be awake and say that, looking around the world today? There are plenty of heartbreaking, devastating events, and that's true personally and globally. Pain is part of life, and to deny that is to live in a dream-world full of unicorns and glitter, with an occasional leprechaun running through.

Another really popular saying: "Everything is happening for a reason." I always cringe when I see that, because years ago, in another lifetime, I said that myself. Then I got older and saw some things and went through some things, and realized that's an awful thing to say, even though I meant well when I said it. It's an awful thing to say, because you never know who you're saying it to, especially if you say it in a room full of students you don't know personally, or you post it on social media to friends you don't know. What if there's a grieving parent in the room, or on your newsfeed? Do you think they're going to take any kind of comfort in that idea, or do you think you might have inadvertently alienated them, leaving them to feel even more alone and angry than they already did? I'm not saying you can't believe that, I'm saying it isn't a compassionate thing to say.

"Everything is perfect and unfolding exactly the way I need it to for my soul to evolve. This moment is offering me everything I need to know." Get me the f&cking toothpicks. When we speak in these terms, we're suggesting there's a divine plan, and a certain path that's been designed just for us, so that we can get the lessons we need. And maybe you believe that. Maybe you believe in karmic inheritance and reincarnation. I'd love to believe that. I'd love to believe we get more than one crack at this thing. I'd love to believe that some of the devastating things that have happened in my life have happened in order to balance out any of my past transgressions, and to help my soul evolve in this lifetime. I mean, reincarnation is such a comforting idea. We get to come back, and maybe we even get to travel with the same souls, we get to be with our loved ones again? That would make death a lot less scary, right? And I mean, we know energy doesn't die, it just changes form, so who knows? We're energy. And I believe in the continuation of consciousness, because that makes sense to me, and because I want to. But I don't know for sure what happens after this, and neither does anyone else, and I'm not going to pretend differently. And because I don't know for sure, I'm not going to say things with confidence that might not be true.

Anyway. Here's the other problem with that line of thinking. If you believe everything is happening for a reason, you're probably also going to treat the trials and challenges of your life as some kind of test. You're going to ask yourself, "Why is this happening to me?" In other words, you'll relinquish your own power. Sometimes we exaggerate our own importance, and sometimes we dishonor it. I mean, there are about 7 billion of us on this planet. Each of us unique. So right off the bat, we're going to have 7 billion distinct experiences, but there's universality, right? I mean, talk to people. We're a lot more the same than we are different. We all dream. We all long for connection, love, touch, understanding, compassion, forgiveness and acceptance. We all have our heartbreaks, our unfulfilled wishes, nights when we've cried ourselves to sleep. We all feel alone in this gig from time to time, on the outside looking in, when really, we're on the inside looking out.

If you see a pattern in your life, if you keep making choices that lead to your heartbreak, I'd take a good, hard look at that. Then the question is not, "Why is this happening to me?", but, "Why does this pattern keep showing up, why do I keep making these choices, and what is this pattern trying to reveal to me?" Because that way, you're acknowledging your free will, and your own power. Things are not just happening to us. Life brings its everything, and we respond. We co-write this story.

Sometimes people do crappy things because they're young and selfish, or they don't know themselves well, or they grow in a different direction, or they can't face what they want so they make a mess. You don't have to be on the receiving end of poor treatment, wondering where the lesson is for you. I mean, again, if it keeps happening, then yes, you have to ask yourself why you keep picking people who lack the tools to love you well. But we can all cross paths with a scorpion from time to time. The only lesson in that case is that people in pain, spread pain. That is all.

Letting Go with Love

How do you let go when everything in your being, every cell in your body, has been wired to hold on? The loss of a child, no matter how old, is as bad as it gets. Losing people is the hardest thing we go through as human beings. It's devastating when we're lost from people we don't know how to live without. It's crushing, it's hard to breathe. There's a hole where a universe once existed. It seems impossible the world keeps spinning. Or that people everywhere are getting up and brushing their teeth or driving to work or sending a text as if everything hasn't changed.

I want to say up front that some things are never going to be okay. There are some losses that are so great, you're just going to carry them. That doesn't mean that joy cannot exist again. Or that you won't experience great love, or be filled with gratitude for those moments that come out of nowhere and leave you with tears of appreciation. It's incredible to be alive. It isn't always easy, but it's wildly interesting and life is full of the potential to surprise us and help us to grow and open. Of course there are some ways we'd rather not grow, and some lessons we'd rather not learn. But we don't get to choose. When your heart breaks, it opens and softens and expands, or it hardens and contracts. I highly recommend you allow the pain to open you. But I do not believe you have to be thankful for the opportunity to grow in that way. Not everything in life has to go in the "thank you" column.

Sometimes we lose people because they choose to leave us. This kind of pain happens between parents and children, between siblings, between best friends. I think it's incredibly sad when family members stop speaking to one another. I recognize sometimes that's the only way to heal and move on. If there's physical or verbal abuse, if there's addiction, if there's a personality disorder that results in a person who's unable to empathize or communicate with any kind of compassion, then you may not have a choice. But short of that, it breaks my heart when I hear about families ripped apart.

I met a woman at a holiday party one year, and we started talking. Before long, she told me she has two sons, but she's only in contact with one of them, her youngest. He was also at the party. She said her other son had married a woman who just didn't like her. From the beginning, no matter what she did, it was wrong, or not good enough. And her son was in the middle, and his wife got pregnant, and the longer they were together, the less he found ways to communicate.

She'd tried apologizing to her son, and owning anything she could think of, she'd told him how much she missed him. She'd never met her grandchild. She said she had been a single mom, she'd raised the boys on her own. She certainly hadn't been perfect, but she'd always done her best. Her younger son came over at one point. He put his arm around her, and kissed her on top of her head. When she went to get food, he told me his brother had married a very unhappy woman, and that he was sure his brother wasn't happy with the situation. But he also told me his mother was one in a million. Always there for them. Working her ass off to make sure they always had what they needed, and most of what they wanted. And that he was furious his brother was treating her so poorly. So it had taken a tremendous toll on their relationship as well. He'd asked his brother what their mother had possibly done to be in a situation where she doesn't even get to meet her grandchild? And his brother's response was to shut down their communication as well.

What do you do in a mess like that? It's heartbreaking. You cannot force people to be open or rational or kind or compassionate. They are those things, or they are not. Sometimes people are weak, or they're insecure, or they doubt their worth on a core level, and then they get involved with a strong personality who takes over. Controlling people are attracted to fragile people. I don't know enough about the woman and her sons to have any real sense of what was going on there, but you have a grown man who was abandoned by his father as a small child. And maybe some part of him has always felt doubtful about his worth. If your own parent can leave you, you must be pretty unlovable, right? Like I said, I can't swear that was this guy's thing, but I've heard from so many people over the years, and I can tell you from my own personal experience, if you don't heal your deep wounds, they bite you in the ass again and again. They break your heart until you can't see straight. And you become so lost to yourself, it's easier to let other people make decisions for you, tell you where to go and how to be, how to think, and who to see. I mean, that isn't a life, that's a fog. But a lot of people exist that way, and you can't march into the center of that fog and wake them up. They do that on their own, or they don't.

It hurts like hell when someone revises history and turns you into a person you don't recognize. It's even worse when your own child does that. The person you bathed and fed and strapped into car seats. The person who's lunch you made and breakfast and dinner, too, for years and years and years. The person whose hand you held, and knees you bandaged and face you gazed into, and saw the moon and the stars and the sun, all at once. The little person you read to and laughed with and fought for and sat up with through sickness and heartbreak and mean kids at school. Of course it hurts to have that person discard you, deny you, reject you. And it isn't easy to go through the day and know that person is going about his business. That you could pick up the phone and hear his voice, or get in your car and see his face. Except you can't, because you've been invited to disappear.

All you can do is communicate your love, your pain, your confusion, and your desire for connection. Once you're sure you've done that, I think you have to do your best to let go with love. Hopefully, your child will find his or her way back to you. Hopefully, eventually, the fog will lift. The pain of being in a false reality will outweigh the pain of healing and making things right. Until then, you have to do your best to remember who you are. To forgive yourself your imperfections, because we all have them, and not one of us gets it right in every moment. You have to do what you can to remove the onus of guilt and blame if they don't belong to you.

That woman at the party told me she must have failed as a mother, to have a son who could do this, but I don't agree. Maybe he needed help. Maybe he was in more pain than she knew or understood. Maybe she was so stressed out trying to make ends meet for herself and two boys, she missed some signs. Being exiled is a harsh punishment. After twenty-five, we are responsible for how we behave and what we do. And I'm being generous. Really, twenty-five is old enough to know how to treat people. It's old enough to get help with your healing process; it's old enough to recognize that you need help. It's old enough to tell your boyfriend or girlfriend or spouse that no one comes between you and the people you love. And this guy was way over twenty-five.

Blaming and shaming and pointing fingers is a sad way to go through life. Being so unsure of your worth that you allow someone else to dictate the terms of your day and your relationships is a prison sentence. Having your heart broken by one of the two people you treasure most in the world is incredibly sad. But these things happen. All you can do is try your best to build joy around the fracture. The fault line is there, there's no denying it. But doing your best to be kind to yourself, to gravitate toward love, to reassure yourself of reality when you need to, these are all things you can do. If the situation permits, maybe every so often you reach out. You stick with the throughline of love, and leave it at that. You take your life day by day, which is all any of us can do, anyway. And you figure out what you can do to nurture yourself on this day. What you can do to uplift the people around you. What you can do that will bring you joy and peace and fulfillment. And you carve out some time for those things. Talking to people really helps. Sharing your story, finding support, being with people who know how to hold a space for your grief without trying to make it better, those things are all helpful. Hopefully one day your child or your parent or your sibling will realize life is short and time is precious. Holding on to rage when you could be opening to love won't serve anyone.

Give it Time

Sometimes our expectations of ourselves are so unrealistic. We have ideas about how we should feel, or where we should be at any given point in time, and if we aren't meeting those markers, we feel disappointed in ourselves, or frustrated, or we wonder what's wrong with us. This comes up a lot around grieving, mourning, and recovering from heartbreak of any kind. There's no timer for this stuff; there's no formula. It's different for everyone, and dependent upon so many factors. But the last thing you need when you're suffering, is to feel badly about yourself because you aren't done suffering quickly enough.

Obviously it's no fun to be pining or longing or missing people we cherish. Death is the most extreme version of this, of course. Grieving has no time limit. As rabbi, bereavement counselor, and author Earl Grollman says, "The only cure for grief is to grieve." No matter how much we understand we'll all die eventually, it's still almost incomprehensible when someone we love is ripped from us. It's natural to want to hug the people we love, to hear their voices, their laughter, to hold their hands. The loss of a person is like the loss of a whole, beautiful world. There's a shock to it, it seems impossible that the earth could keep spinning. And depending upon who's been lost to you, and in what way they were taken, and at what point in your life and theirs, the impact may bring you to your knees.

The only thing at a time like that, is to ask for help.

Hopefully, you don't even have to do that. Hopefully the people in your life know how to show up for you, at least some of them. So that you know you aren't alone. But for many people, grief is difficult to witness, because it reminds them of their own mortality, the fragility of life, and the potential that they, too, could have to hold a sorrow so great. The people who are the most uncomfortable holding a space for your pain, are likely the same people who will tell you you "should be feeling better by now." What they're really saying is, "I'm having a hard time being around you when you're in pain, and I'd like you to make it easier for me."

The thing is, when you're mourning, your only job is to allow yourself to feel whatever you need to feel, for as long as you need to feel it. Anyone who can't honor that or understand it is probably not going to be one of your cronies when you're ninety-five, sipping lemonade in your rocker. But you don't need tons of close friends. You just need a few.

The same goes for the loss of any relationship. You have to factor in all kinds of things. How much time and energy you invested, how many memories, shared experiences, heartaches and growing pains you went through. If you had a family with this person, it gets exponentially more complicated. But even if we're talking about someone you dated for a few months, having a broken heart never feels good. You just have to give yourself time. Examine what happened, especially if you're disappointed with the way you showed up, but try not to obsess. Glean the information from the experience that's going to help you grow, and make different choices the next time.

If you're recovering from a toxic relationship, understand your oldest, deepest wounds were probably in play, and that it's very likely you could use some support. It might be a great time to find a good therapist, and do some deep and needed work toward healing. But don't beat yourself up because you aren't over your ex. Some days will be better than others, and these are just natural feelings. Don't stalk their social media making yourself sick, and try not to invest too much of your time or energy wondering what they're doing. Focus on your own healing. As author and inspirational speaker Regina Brett says, you have to, "Give time, time." You know that anything you resist, persists. Of course we don't want to marinate in pain, but denying it or running from it or numbing it out just prolongs the inevitable. Eventually you have to face it, and the more you're willing to acknowledge and work with your pain, the faster you'll move through it. But I can't give you any specific time-frame, and neither can anyone else.

What I can say, is reach out if you need support. Be kind to yourself. Gravitate toward people who don't try to fix things or tell you how to feel, but are simply able to listen and to be there. Nurture yourself, and spend time doing those things that bring you joy and fulfillment. Volunteer if you have it in you. Try to move your body and sweat and breathe once a day. Weep. Feed yourself well, and I don't just mean food—pay attention to what you're watching, reading, telling yourself. And try to have patience. One day, you'll wake up, and the weight and heaviness of your grief won't come crashing down upon you as you blink your eyes open and remember where you are. In the meantime, have some compassion for yourself. Life is a constant lesson in impermanence and loss. There's also incredible beauty and joy and love. But it isn't easy.

CHAPTER 8: OLD WOUNDS, CURRENT PROBLEMS

Whenever we refuse to acknowledge our pain, it swims beneath the surface of everything we do, rising up to bite us in the ass again and again. Old childhood wounds shape us and inform the way we look at the world, and the way we think about ourselves, and sometimes the things we've learned need to be unlearned. This is how we free ourselves and open up new ways of being and thinking about things, but there's no way to do that if we aren't willing to sit with our pain and understand ourselves.

That's How the Light Gets In

I remember the morning my mom told me my dad didn't live with us anymore. I was almost four, and we were sitting at the dining room table at breakfast, and she told me he was going to be living somewhere else, and that eventually I would visit him there. I went into their bedroom, and looked through all his drawers and closets. His denim shirts were gone, his sun lamp was gone, and so were the styrofoam heads that held his different wigs; he was an actor. When I saw he'd left his robe, I thought he'd have to come back, but I was wrong.

It had been a confusing time already. My beloved grandma had died the week before, and I'd been too young to visit in her hospital room that last day, which was probably good. I remember my grandma laughing, and hugging me, full of life. But suddenly it seemed people were disappearing, and not peripheral players, either. We'd seen my grandma almost every day of my life. She and my mom were really close. She and I were really close. It amazes me to think about the impact she's had on my life, and to realize I didn't even get four full years with her. And now my dad had gone to some unknown place, and I had no real sense of time. I don't know how my mom got through that conversation with me without crying.

For years, I lived in fear of being left. I didn't realize I was doing this, of course, but it's obvious in the rear-view mirror. I tried to be a good girl. I thought if I got straight-A's and looked right and behaved well, then maybe I'd be safe, and that followed me into my adulthood. I entered into relationships with people not thinking about what I wanted or needed, or even if I was having fun, but almost solely focused on how I could be perfect for them. How I could make myself indispensable. Un-leave-able.

I'm sharing this with you not because it's a heartbreaking tale. I hear worse stories every day. Lots of people get divorced (not that it makes it easy on the children involved), lots of people lose their grandparents. The proximity in my case was unfortunate because it was like a bomb went off, or an earthquake shook the foundation of what I'd known, but my parents had been keeping up appearances because my grandma was sick that last year, and they didn't want her to worry. I know someone who watched his father die at eight years old while they were playing. I know someone who's dad left when she was seven and never looked back. I can't even wrap my head around how you could leave your kid and never look back. And then there are stories of abuse and neglect and all kinds of things that would leave you on your knees. My point in sharing is that our pain does not just magically disappear. If we don't examine it when we become conscious adults, it swims beneath the surface of everything we do, wreaking havoc on our lives. And life doesn't have to be that way. We all want to heal. We all want to be happy. We wrote it into our Declaration of Independence, so there's not much doubt that we value happiness. It's just that the large majority of us will seek to heal in all the ways that make things worse.

Because we long to heal, we call into our lives those dynamics that reflect our deepest wounds. Mostly, we don't even know we're doing that. If you're afraid of being left, you probably have an excellent, uncanny, perverse knack for picking people who struggle to commit. This is no coincidence, because, presto! Now you have your chance to heal, right? All you have to do is get your partner to want to be with you, and that will be the balm for your original wound. Except it won't, because if you pick people who struggle to commit, you set yourself up to be left again, thus confirming your deepest fear that you are the kind of person it's easy to leave. Or worse, that you just aren't worthy of love. You're leave-able, not lovable.

There's the hard, long road, and there's the hard, short road. I'm not going to lie about that, those are the choices. I mean, those are the choices unless you happen to be one of the three people in the world who had idyllic childhoods. And even if you are, someone else has probably come along and broken your heart by now. Chances are, you have some issues, some stuff to work through like any other human. And it's not a level playing field as I mentioned above, so what you'll need to heal, and how long it will take and what tools you'll use are all personal. But avoiding that work is a surefire way to prolong your pain and allow unconscious drives to rule your life. The longer you wait, the longer you suffer. There's no reason your past has to screw up your present. You are not stuck in a time-warp.

It took me a long time and a lot of work to get right with myself, and it's still a daily practice, but at this point, I'm in the maintenance part. Of course things come up that might tap an old wound, but the wounds have scar tissue, they aren't raw and bleeding, and they aren't unknown to me. They're almost like old, familiar friends. Ah, fear of abandonment. I feel you. I see you. I tip my hat to you. But you don't own me anymore.

If you're an adult, and you've had enough time as an adult to recognize patterns in your life that aren't serving you, I'd get on that. Tools that have worked for me are a daily yoga practice (and I mean all eight limbs), seated meditation, and therapy.

I've also read some tremendously helpful books, and I've done quite a lot of journaling. There are so many tools available. It's my personal belief that it isn't a luxury to pursue healing modalities until you find a mix that works for you; I believe it's your responsibility. You have this life. You have a body. You have time and energy. These things are all gifts. Then, there are your own, particular gifts that are born of your own experiences and perspective and ways of looking at the world. There's only one of you. So if you don't figure out how to set yourself free, you rob the world of gifts only you can bring to it. And that would be a tremendous shame.

Be Your Own Clean-Up Crew

Sometimes we get ourselves into difficult situations, and find we really want a way out, but the way does not seem clear. This is really common when we're young. I certainly got myself into some tight spots along the way, and made a mess on the way out. Part of it is just that it takes time to know ourselves. It's very easy to go through the first quarter of our lives being influenced by external factors. We might place a lot of value on what other people want for us. How other people want us to be or to feel. We might feel pressured by societal norms, or the way our friends seem to be doing things. There are countless ways to get lost on the path.

When I say "the path", I'm not suggesting there's one path for everyone. I mean, your particular path. The one that's going to lead to your deepest, truest self. The one that's going to take you to your joy so you can swim in it and share it. The thing is, we aren't encouraged to look inward, we're taught to focus outside ourselves and meet certain markers. And those markers might differ from family to family, and from culture to culture, but we all have them. The expectations, the ingrained beliefs and ideas about things. Sometimes we have a lot of unlearning to do to figure out what makes sense to us, to uncover what scares us, inspires us, excites us. And if you haven't figured that out and you go ahead and make huge life decisions before you know who you are, you're pretty much guaranteed to crash into some brick walls, and hurt yourself and others. As long as you aren't reckless with other people, as long as you don't set out to hurt anyone, no one can hate you for being young and confused. For thinking you want something, and then getting it, only to find out it is not what you thought it would be. That's called being young and making mistakes, and it's how we grow and learn.

Having said all of that, your choices and your actions define you, as does the way you make your mistakes, and the way you address them. What you do about how you feel is the stuff of character-building. Making a mistake is no crime. Handling it in a cruel or unkind way, leaving someone in the dark, showing a lack of compassion and empathy—those things are crimes. They're crimes against your own heart and your own well-being, in addition to the harm you're inflicting on the other party. The human heart is resilient, and most people will recover from heartbreak, abandonment or betrayal, given enough time, and assuming they avail themselves of tools that help with healing. Having to live with the fact that you treated someone poorly, though, that's another thing. At night, in your bed, when all the noise of the day stops and you're left with your thoughts and your internal dialogue, there's nowhere to hide. You can't run from yourself. You have to be able to live in your own skin, and breathe.

But sometimes we get desperate and it's hard to face the mess we've made and so we try to run or hide or deny or deflect. And of course, that just compounds the pain and confusion, and lengthens the time it will take to heal. You cannot heal in murky waters, and you cannot heal if you lie to yourself. The sooner you face your problems head on, the sooner life will feel good again. It's funny. Years ago I was on a play date with my son. He was about four. And when we were leaving, I told him to go and help his friend clean up the mess of toys they'd created. And the other mom said her housekeeper would do it, and that she preferred that anyway, because she didn't want to end up with a nerdy kid who wore a pocket protector. I said I didn't want to create a grown man who left his dishes and dirty laundry all over the house for his wife to pick up. I didn't say it as a challenge, it just kind of slipped out. And we looked at each other and laughed. And she sent both of our boys to go clean up. Often I see dog poop on the street. It's the same syndrome. If you go through life expecting other people to clean up the messes you've made, don't expect to be happy, because part of being happy requires that we're accountable, that we've taken ownership of the way we're going to show up in the world. Sometimes in an effort to help someone, we rob them of the opportunity to do that. Instead of helping, we're enabling behavior that's weakening to this person we love. And true love doesn't weaken us. It strengthens us.

Take Off the Armor

There comes a time when you really have to put down the blame and the sad stories and take ownership of your life, and your own happiness. You can't point fingers and expect to feel good, because you're making yourself powerless, and that feels terrible. You can't feed your despair and also wonder why you aren't happy. We are all here for a blink of time. It's not how long we have, although I hope we all have long and healthy lives, it's what we do with the time we're gifted. Stoking the flames of your rage and bitterness would be an awful way to go.

There are so many people living in fear. Maybe it's the vulnerability of being human that terrifies them, but it seems they've decided a shield of anger is better than an open heart. Usually when you're dealing with that kind of armor, it's because the heart it's protecting was so badly broken. The thing is, those breaks can harden us or soften us. Softening feels a lot better. I know people personally who seem determined to die angry, though. It's almost like they want their tombstone to read, "My life was hard, and it wasn't my fault", with a list of people at fault underneath.

You can't cuddle up with the "last word." If you choose being right over being at peace, it's going to be a long and lonely road. Sometimes people are afraid to put down the sad story, because who are they without it? I once met a woman with blazing eyes who told me she could not forgive her father because then he wouldn't pay for what he'd done. But she hadn't spoken to him in years. So who's paying? I mean, some things are unforgivable. Sometimes you have to choose not to have someone in your life. But you can do that with rage or acceptance.

Pain makes us grow. The butterfly needs the struggle out of the cocoon to strengthen its wings. If you cut open the cocoon, it will never fly. We need the travel down the birth canal to squeeze the fluid out of our lungs so we can breathe easily. If you've never suffered, you can't help people who are in pain, because pain creates empathy. Sometimes people have blinders on and they actually think their story is unique, but you know what? I hear stories from people every single day and they're the same. Something happens when we're young. Maybe we aren't received with love. Maybe we learn the world is unsafe and our best bet is to be invisible or indispensable, or both, depending on the minute or the day. Maybe those experiences create doubt within us. Doubt about our own worth. That's a very common story. That, and fear of abandonment. Also, people suffering over betrayal, abuse, cruelty. Almost every time I post someone says, "This was exactly what I needed to hear today." Or, "Are you psychic?" I'm not psychic. We're so much more the same than we are different.

Your memories are yours. Your ideas, your experiences, your frame of reference, the way you've come to perceive the people and the world around you, all of these are unique to you, but if you start talking to people you will also find the themes are uncannily similar. The pain and struggles and fears and doubts and failures we face are universal. How we respond to them defines us.

Life is full of moments that are so gorgeous they suck the air out of your lungs and make your heart expand simultaneously. There are events that will undoubtedly put you on the ground with your mouth full of dirt and your head full of why. In the world right now, there are bombs going off, shots being fired. Children are dying, or they're watching their parents die. These things are happening and it's hard to bear witness and there are no easy answers. Sometimes people are ripped from us when we aren't done loving them. We aren't done. It's not a level playing field. Some people will suffer in ways that make your own heart ache. Don't think you're the only one. You're not alone in this.

The thing is, you have a spark that is yours alone. And you can feed that spark until it becomes a roaring fire in your heart, and lights you up from the inside. And you can give that fire that's yours, you can give that away every day. Whether it's a fire of rage or a fire of love is up to you. But I think we have enough rage in the world. Healing is a lot easier than being bitter and angry and isolated for eighty, ninety or one hundred years. When I say healing, that's personal. What you'll need to heal is something only you can determine. But I'd get on that, because life is ticking away right now, this minute. And I don't say that without compassion. It takes a lot of bravery to release an old story.

I tried life the angry way. I pointed fingers and made my unhappiness and frustration and disappointment the fault of other people, but it wasn't. Things happen and they shape you, but none of us is frozen in time unless we choose to be. The earth keeps spinning, and it will continue to do so long after we're gone. Take hold of the one thing you can—how you're going to show up, what you're going to offer. May all beings be free from suffering.

Stop the Cycle

Sometimes we get into a pattern with someone that just isn't serving our highest good, or theirs. This happens a lot with toxic relationships. Usually, something in the dynamic is harkening back to old wounds for both parties. We're driven to heal, but often, we go about it in all the wrong ways.

Unacknowledged pain swims below the surface of everything we do, and until we bring this stuff into the light, we'll keep calling it into our lives in unconscious ways. You know when you feel triggered by someone? There's an excellent chance they're hitting a painful nerve. The thing is, when we attract people into our spheres so we can play out an ancient drama, we also attract people who are going to be very unlikely to help us rewrite the script.

If your dad left when you were four and you have abandonment issues you haven't dealt with, it's likely you're going to be attracted to men or women who can't commit. That way, your fear of being left is now in play, and you can go about the business of trying to claim your prize and procure your happy ending, by getting your partner to be "yours." But a person who has trouble committing is going to run like hell from that scenario. It could be they grew up feeling smothered by one parent or the other, so they're both attracted and repelled by your neediness. We want to overcome those feelings and situations we couldn't master as children, and our attachment styles play a big role in how we go about trying to do that.

Anyway, the point is, you won't heal this way, you'll just relive that old pain, and throw salt in a wound you've never addressed. You'll take your partner's inability to commit to you (or whatever issue it is you keep replaying), as a sign that you are in fact, unlovable, or easy to leave, or invisible, or whatever it is you fear the most, when the truth is, they have their own story and their own wounds. A person with fear of commitment fears all commitment. It's what you represent, it isn't you they're rejecting. But that doesn't matter, because if your heart is broken, it's broken.

You'll save yourself a lot of time and heartache if you simply face your pain. If you notice you keep repeating patterns in your life with family members, friends, partners, colleagues and strangers, it's time to get some help. Identifying your issues is half the battle. You don't want to get stuck there. You want to be able to rewire the system, and put a time-stamp on those things from your past that are still haunting you today. If you had a parent who overpowered you or made love a conditional thing, you don't have to be afraid of intimacy for the rest of your life. You can work with your fear. You can meet it head on. You can be aware of it without acting on it. But it takes work, and you'll almost definitely need support.

I highly recommend the combination of yoga and therapy. Therapy to me is the "top-down" part. You identify your issues and get really clear about your tendencies, weak spots, and potential pitfalls. Yoga is the "bottom-up" part. You get in your body and you breathe. Whatever your tendencies are, believe me they'll follow you onto your mat. Yoga is confrontational by nature. You'll get to deal with your habitual responses to challenge, frustration, and intense, uncomfortable sensation.

Intense emotions create intense sensations—deal with this on your mat, and you'll be able to deal with it in your life. Over time, when you feel triggered, you'll be able to breathe through those feelings without acting on them— running out the door, or lashing out, or saying or doing things you'll later regret. Now you're not stuck in the identification phase, you're actually taking ownership of your issues, and refusing to let your past ruin your present and future. If you have a loud inner critic, you'll become aware of that, and in so doing, you'll give yourself the power to starve it. You'll get to rewire your system from the ground up. Does it take dedication and determination? Yes. Is it easy? No. But you know what's a lot harder? Not doing it and replaying your pain like you're in a real-life version of "Groundhog's Day." Great movie, but no way to move through life. Break the cycle and create something new for yourself that feels good. I'd trade short-term pain and discomfort for a lifetime of suffering any day of the week.

Free Yourself and Forgive

Sometimes I write about forgiveness and people get very upset. I recognize there are some things we want to put into the category of unforgivable, so let me clarify what I mean when I say I believe forgiveness is freeing and vital if you want to be at peace. I am not talking about deciding that something traumatic or hurtful that happened in your past is now okay with you. I'm not talking about picking up the phone or sending an email to a person who betrayed you, and telling them it's water under the bridge. You don't have to tell anyone. You don't have to speak to the person, or see them ever again. But if you're holding onto anger, they're still hurting you, and that's my point.

When we're enraged with someone, we're carrying them around inside our heads and our hearts. Because whatever happened is in the past, but in order for us to stay angry, we have to keep thinking about it, and fueling that flame. And rage is a poor constant companion. It seeps into everything. It makes it hard for us to be intimate, to trust other people, to let our guard down, because to do that, you have to be vulnerable, but to hold onto rage, you have to be tough. And staying angry requires constant vigilance; it's exhausting. We end up depleting our energy on that, when we could be spending it on opening to love, which feels so much better.

How do you forgive someone who stole any chance you had at a normal, innocent childhood, for example? That's a difficult one, right? Because something was taken from you, and you can never have it back. You can never know what it would have been like to be in Kindergarten feeling safe and secure. You can never know how it might have felt if you'd been able to relate to kids your age, not just in Kindergarten, but in elementary school, junior high, high school, college. It turns out not having a childhood affects you for your whole life. So how do you forgive that? You can re-parent yourself. That little kid who was scared and confused and hurt and alienated is still available to you, and you already know that. If you're an adult, you aren't powerless anymore, and it's never too late to heal. Maybe you get yourself some help, some support. In fact, I'd highly recommend you do that.

Healing takes dedication, time, energy, and a willingness to lean into your pain. If you refuse to work with your issues, don't expect them to get tired and go away. They'll just keep showing up for you in every area of your life. They'll be bubbling right under the surface of everything you say and do. If you face your fears, your rage, your loss, your grief, if you allow yourself to mourn, you'll find you don't mourn forever. The deep feelings arise, and they hurt, and you cry and you feel raw and maybe some days you feel hopeless or alone or scared, but you hang on. And eventually the heat and the power and the strength of all that old stuff starts to subside, and you can loosen your grip and start to breathe again, maybe for the first time in a very long time.

It's just, if you're using a ton of energy to stay angry, you're probably not going to have enough left to heal. Blame keeps us stuck. It places our ability to be happy in someone else's hands, or in events over which we had, and have, no control. The past can't be rewritten; whatever happened, happened. Some things shape us, but the only thing that defines you is what you do about what you've been given. How you proceed. How you live your life, and show up for yourself, and the people you love, and the people you don't even know. Forgiveness is a gift you give to yourself. It has very little to do with anyone else.

Sometimes people balk at the word forgiveness, so let me say this. If you're living your life and you're happy and you don't feel like you're carrying within your heart someone who betrayed you, then I think you're good to go. You don't have to call that forgiveness, but that's what it is in my book. You are not a prisoner of another person's actions or inactions; you're liberated.

And the same goes for people who enter our lives later in life. Maybe you had an idyllic childhood, but something unthinkable happened later. This is your life. You get to decide how much energy you're going to spend looking back. If you work on it enough, you can witness your experience. You can examine your thinking. You can choose one thought over another. And there's so much power in that. Choose the thoughts that strengthen you. Feed the love. Let the rest of it go, as much as you can. It doesn't have to fit into a neat little box. You certainly don't have to be grateful for everything that's ever happened to you. Just grow from your pain. Allow it to soften you and make you more insightful and compassionate, and likely to reach out to other people in pain. That way, at least, some beauty grows from it. Learn to love yourself as you are right now, and understand, you wouldn't be you without every event that's ever befallen you. Remind yourself that you're strong, and unhook your journey from someone else's past behavior. That's their journey, it isn't yours.

You Take the Keys

When I was in college I had a roommate for one semester, I'll call her Jane. I didn't know her, we were just placed in a room together. Jane liked boys. A lot. I walked in on Jane with so many different Tarzans, we finally devised a system where she'd leave a post-it note on the door. Not that Jane was ever troubled if I showed up in the middle of her eggs being scrambled, I just found it awkward. And Jane was annoyed by the fact that I found it awkward.

When I wasn't interrupting something, I'd come back to our room and find sweaters of mine thrown in a corner, sometimes stained, or I'd go looking for a pair of shoes only to discover Jane must be wearing them. She was catty, and cold, and never had a kind word to say about anyone, not that she talked to me much. I tried to get to know her, but she really wasn't open to that, nor did she have any other girlfriends. If I saw her on campus, she was almost always with a group of guys, and might acknowledge me with a look, but not a friendly one, and not usually. One morning I walked into our tiny shared kitchen and howled because I stepped on a shard of broken glass. Jane had knocked over a vase, and simply thrown a towel over the mess. Finally, frustrated and done, I requested a new roommate. The paperwork took a few weeks, but there was light at the end of the tunnel.

One afternoon after I knew my days with Jane were coming to an end, I walked in to find her alone in her bed. She looked awful, her cheeks were flushed, her eyes were glassy and she was groaning. She had the kind of flu where you just want to dig a hole and bury yourself until it's over. Her fever was incredibly high, but she refused to let me take her to the nurse. So I went to the store and bought soup and juice and bread for toast, and came back and made her a little lunch. I sat on the edge of the bed and put my hand on her forehead, and Jane started crying. Not just a tear or two streaming down her face, but the kind of crying that sounds more like keening. Primal, deep wailing. I was stunned, but I just held onto her until she quieted.

It turned out Jane's mom had left when she was a baby, and never looked back. Her dad had raised her but he wasn't the most emotional guy. No one had ever made her soup before. I wish I could say this was the beginning of a close and lasting friendship, or tell you that I still know Jane and that all is well with her. But that moment with the soup was all there was, because the next day Jane was back to her dismissive ways. In fact, she was even more hostile. When I packed up my things before winter break, I left Jane a card with my new phone number and a note that said she could always call me for any reason. I never heard from her, but I think about her a lot. Especially when I meet someone who's challenging to be around, or whose behavior is difficult to understand. Everyone has pain, everyone is struggling with something.

When you feel as though someone is "driving you cra-

ALLY HAMILTON

zy," understand they can only do that if you let them. Checking in with yourself when you're feeling enraged, frustrated, trapped, or shut down with someone is really essential. Sometimes a complete stranger can "drive you crazy" by talking loudly on their cellphone in a cafe, or not holding a door open, or not letting you merge on the freeway. Sometimes it's someone you like who isn't responding the way you wish they would. The story that matters is always the story of our participation. What about the situation is triggering us? Why, for example, would you allow the driving habits of a stranger, no matter how annoying they might be, to rob you of your own peace? Or affect your blood pressure, or the way you're driving, or what you're doing with your own middle finger? What is the real source of the anger, or insecurity, or lack of trust this person is tapping that already exists within you, and did long before s/he came into the picture? If you're really tweaked, consider whether it's old stuff. Are you feeling powerless? Rejected? Abandoned? Are you repeating a pattern of interaction that feels awful and very familiar at the same time? This is the way challenging people can become some of our best teachers.

The potential for growth and greater understanding about who you are and where you're at is always available. If someone cuts you off on the freeway and you feel a surge of heat rush to your face, you really ought to be yelling, "Thank you!" and not, "F&ck you!" out the window, because they just helped you release and explore some of the rage that was already within you. Next time you're dreading hanging out with that person who drives you up and down a wall, see if you can turn it into an experiment where you drive instead. They can do and say anything at all, and you will still drive your own car, peacefully and mindfully, slowing down whenever you need to hop out and take a few deep breaths.

It's Not You, It's Me

Sometimes the best way to figure out where there may be room for some deep inner healing is to examine patterns in your life. Patterns frequently show up in romantic relationships. If you have not experienced peace and steadiness in your personal life, maybe it's the time to look back and see if there's a theme threading through your history. Are you always trying to save people? Are you attracted to partners who are unavailable in some way? Do you go after people who don't treat you well? Or, are you the one sabotaging your chances for love? Do you run? Do you "check out"? Do you keep finding yourself in the very situation you were trying to avoid?

If you're getting a yes to any of these, or you recognize other patterns, chances are, you have found the thread that can lead you back to some very old, very deep pain. It seems to be a human tendency to try to "rewrite history." Even in day to day life, the mind will get snagged on a conversation that has already happened and try to re-do it, to come up with the "perfect" thing to say, but, there's no potential in the past. It's good to examine it, though, particularly if you feel you might be dragging your past into your present.

If you can identify the "original why" of any patterns you detect, you can take the unconscious repetition out of your future, not that it's easy, speaking from my own experience. But your past does not have to determine your present, or what's on your horizon. If you can bring the source (or sources) of your pain into your consciousness, into your awareness, you take the power away from that inner wiring that may be attracting you to the very situations bound to result in more pain. You can "catch yourself', identify that "old, familiar feeling" that can be mistaken for love, and sit with yourself instead of acting out. Acknowledging and leaning into your pain takes the heat out of it, and that old fire that pulls you to act, even when you know you're heading straight into a brick wall, will start to subside and cool.

Loving yourself is soothing for your soul, it's a salve, and it's a relief. The process of rewiring your system will probably be uncomfortable at best, and it's very easy to slip back into that old groove as you try to head toward something different. Don't beat yourself up if you feel like you must head into another brick wall. Your awareness alone is huge, and beating yourself up will just make the crash even worse. Eventually, the wall will lose it's power over you. There are other paths to take that lead toward love, and that don't end with you in tears. Those are the ones to follow.

CHAPTER 9: ANGER, BETRAYAL AND TAKING THINGS PERSONALLY

We human beings tend to contract from the experiences in life that don't feel good. We cling and we grip, and when life does not unfold as we'd hoped, we suffer, or we try to run, numb, deny or point fingers.

Anger, a perfectly normal human emotion, can be a huge issue for many people. Some struggle with lashing out, others with holding it in--either way, the results are painful.

Most of us will go through challenges and disappointments, and we might feel besieged by the world, as if things are happening to us, in particular. Betrayal, loss, and the sting of despair might put us in the, "Why me?" frame of mind, but that never serves our growth, and it always prolongs our suffering.

Anger Management 101

Many people struggle with handling their anger in healthy ways. Did you ever have an altercation with someone, and let them know you could see they were angry, only to have them yell, "I'm NOT ANGRY!!!"? Have you ever been that person?

Sometimes we deny our anger because what we're really feeling is so much more complex. Underneath anger, there's always pain. We might feel vulnerable or threatened. We might feel deeply hurt. We might be afraid that some of our most raw and unhealed places have been exposed. Maybe we feel disrespected, unseen, or unheard. So when we're angry and we say we aren't, sometimes it's because we're trying to express there's so much more to it, and sometimes it's because we don't want to admit our vulnerability in the moment when we're feeling the most unsafe.

When the nervous system is overwhelmed and we're in a state of "fight or flight", the chances are slim for constructive conversation about what's happening. If your heart is racing and your hands are shaking and you have that shallow chest-breathing happening, you're probably not going to be in a position to identify the nuances of what you're feeling. Also, anger is a perfectly natural, human emotion we'll all experience, but sometimes people push it down, and other times they lash out. Learning to manage our anger in healthy ways so we don't deny the truth of what we're feeling, nor do we do or say things we might regret, is a skill worth working on.

We don't have to be afraid of our own anger, nor do we have to be afraid of anyone else's, assuming they aren't going to become so overwhelmed by it that they're dangerous. Recently, I had the unfortunate and heartbreaking experience of watching a man pull his car over to the side of the road and punch the woman in the passenger seat, who was screaming and yelling, "Don't hit me!" He took off before I could get his license plate, and by the time the police arrived (just two minutes later), he was long gone. If you're in a situation like that, you need support, and you need to leave. We can love people who don't yet know how to manage their anger, but we can't stay with them. Living in fear is not living, and you are not here to be a punching bag for anyone. Your physical safety is not something you can compromise, and someone who hits you, and then apologizes and promises it will never happen again, only to hit you a short time later, needs serious help. The cycle isn't going to end just because you love her or him, or because you want it to.

A lot of people are never taught the tools that help when we're in the midst of intense sensation in the body. Any strong emotion—rage, jealousy, insecurity, anxiety, fear, depression, longing, grief, shame, or being in love—creates incredible, visceral sensations. The body does not lie, so if you're angry, it will show on your face, in your hands, in the way you're moving, breathing, standing. Sometimes we're so upset, we want to let it out, and that is okay. In order for people to know us and see us, they have to be willing to enter the fire with us. If you're going to be close to someone, if you're going to work on real trust and intimacy, you're also going to have to share your deepest fears. This is why it's so important to take your time. It takes quite a while to really know another person. But if you're on that path, then you're going to have to give that family member, close friend or romantic partner access to your interior world. And if you're like most people, not all of it is going to be pretty and full of sunshine and unicorns.

When anger erupts, it's like a volcano in the body. You

have to let the heat out, or you'll scorch and burn from the inside. But how you let it out is the thing. Words can be like daggers, and certain things can never be unsaid or forgotten. The body is full of wisdom and it's full of information. The next time you feel overwhelmed, trapped, cornered, or attacked, try to pause and notice your breath. Notice what's happening in your body. See if you can slow down your breathing. The breath is the only involuntary system in the body that we can effect with our minds, and it's powerful. If you can calm your nervous system in the midst of a storm, you give yourself some power over how you're feeling, and what you do about it. You give yourself some room to choose your response. And that's a gift you give to yourself, and everyone in your life.

Let the Disappointments Strengthen You

Few things feel worse than being used or duped, especially at the hands of someone we believed was a friend, but these things happen in life. Betrayal stings because we trusted, and we were wrong. Not only are we disappointed and sometimes disgusted with the other party, we're also angry with ourselves for not having seen more clearly. Also, when we feel disgusted, it's usually because we are really, really hurt.

The trap in these situations is to ask ourselves, "How can this person have done this to me?", and begin to make our list of all the ways we've shown up and been a great and loyal friend, partner, or colleague. The reality is, it's not about you. This person would do this to anyone in similar circumstances. This is where this person happens to be on his or her path at the present moment. You just crossed paths at an unfortunate time.

Now, how do you wrap your head around that if it's your partner? How not to take it to heart in that scenario? It always takes two. In any relationship, the dynamic exists between the two parties. There's you, your partner, and the space between you, and the relationship lives in that space. You are each responsible for what you contribute, whether it's your care, your attention, your energy, your time, your love, your presence, your patience, compassion and forgiveness, your sense of fun, your willingness to keep learning about the other person, or not so much. You are responsible if you neglected that space, if you stopped looking or caring or listening, if you filled that space with your rage, resentment, boredom, fear, frustration, or if you didn't fill the space at all. That's the part to examine.

A lot of the time, we're taking things personally that have nothing to do with us. If someone behaves in a way that lacks integrity, that's their issue. The part that's personal is the healing you'll have to do if you got stung. Also, it's helpful to remember those times when we did not show up the way we wish we had. No one operates from his or her highest self in every moment. We all make mistakes, we all blow it sometimes. Learning from our mistakes so we can make better ones moving forward is the thing. Practicing forgiveness for ourselves and others creates the environment for change and growth. Don't get me wrong, there are some things that are just over the line. You can forgive people for your own well-being, and still choose not to have them in your life.

And the thing is, life is short and precious. You can get really caught up feeling injured, wronged, victimized, but that's time you'll never have back, and that isn't a stance that's going to serve you. Most people are just doing the best they can with what they've got. Sometimes people are really young, selfish, confused, immature. We've all been those things at some point. No need to take it personally, because it's not a reflection of anything lacking within you. As soon as you can, pick yourself up, because there's a lot of beauty in this world, and there are a lot of wonderful human beings. As far as the people who'd walk through fire for you, don't expect a roomful. Maybe a handful. For sure, one. You can always walk through the fire on your own behalf, and sometimes life asks that of us.

What We Do with What We're Given

Sometimes things happen that turn everything we thought we knew upside down and inside out. Recently, a woman wrote to me because she found out her husband had another family "on the side." She and her husband have a son who's five. She believed their son was her husband's first child, but it turns out he has a daughter a year older. She told me she'd been impressed with her husband's ability to change diapers and his ideas about breastfeeding, and just generally how comfortable he'd been when their son was an infant. She didn't realize he'd been through it before. And when she approached him about wanting a second baby, he told her he really felt he was a "one-and-done" kind of guy, but it turns out he has another son, too. He had a second baby with the other woman.

You might wonder how he was able to pull this off for so many years, but he travels on business all the time, and she never thought to worry. She said she believed they were happy. That in their social circle, they were the couple everyone envied because they were still so romantic and seemingly in love with each other. College sweethearts, the whole fairytale story. She found out because the other woman called her. She didn't want to live in hiding anymore. She wanted to be able to have a normal life. She wanted to post pictures of her kids on Facebook, and go to school gatherings with the father of her children. I mean, it was only a matter of time before this whole thing exploded. The kids are getting older. He has three children calling him Daddy, in two different states.

Anyway, it's a total mess. And clearly, this man needs some serious help. I don't know enough about him, his background, his pain, his mental condition, and nine hundred other factors to even begin to comment on what could drive a person to wreak havoc on so many lives, including his own.

The wife is reeling. She's trying to keep it together for the sake of her son. She told her husband to get out, and she called a lawyer. But it's the emotional part that's brutal. A lawyer can't help you negotiate an earthquake that shakes the foundation of your life. That makes you search back and relive every moment that didn't quite add up, to replay every conversation, to find the thread that began to unravel when you didn't notice. In addition to a lawyer, she also called a therapist, her entire family, and her closest friends. She asked me to write about it. She needs support, and she's reaching out, which is good.

Obviously, this is an extreme example, but most of us have experienced betrayal of some kind, or we've been blindsided when something ended and we just did not see it coming, or we thought we knew someone and it turns out we didn't, not really. The hardest part in all of that is feeling like you cannot trust your own judgement, but that's what happens when something rocks the core of everything you believed you could count on. Was my marriage real? Was anything he said real? Was the love real? Was the family real? I'm looking at this and it looks purple, but is it? I mean, you just can't trust anything anymore.

The key toward putting your world back together in

times like those is just to take it one breath at a time, and to allow yourself to feel whatever you need to feel. Heartbroken. Enraged, astounded, depressed, scared. She told me she feels ashamed and humiliated, amongst many other emotions. We talked about the shame part. I told her there's never any shame in loving all the way, and trusting and giving. There is a clear lack of self-respect when someone lies and betrays and sneaks around, and I told her those are things her soon-to-be ex-husband will have to grapple with, but she has nothing to feel ashamed about.

Humiliation is another thing, though. That word comes from the Latin "humus", which means ground, soil, or earth. As if we're being returned to the ground, to the dirt. And I've felt that way before myself. As much as we wouldn't wish it on ourselves or anyone else, there's something freeing about being returned to the earth, and about questioning everything. I'm definitely not suggesting this is some blessing in disguise, although clearly she's been building her life with a person who has deep-rooted problems, I'm just saying once she allows herself the time and space to grieve and heal, she can start to build something new. She can begin again, from the ground up. And there's no doubt this experience is going to make her grow and open and strengthen in ways she wouldn't have without it. It always comes down to what we do with what we're given.

Life is full of curve-balls, and many people are in unfathomable pain. There are also beautiful people in this world who would never, ever betray you, and there are experiences that take your breath away with the sheer force of their awesomeness. We never know what life has in store for us. It is humbling, but it's also interesting and amazing. Whatever's happening in your world, remember there's only one you in the known universe. Only one. Feed your spark, and try to trust in your process. Leave room for life to show up with the joy, too.

Don't Consent to Poor Treatment

Not all friendships or romantic relationships will stand the test of time, and that is okay. Of course it hurts, but it's just the way of things. People change, circumstances change, everything in the universe is in constant motion. Sometimes we think something is "for life", but it turns out not to be. Certain people are going to become "somebody that you used to know." Yes, you can thank me for having that song stuck in your head for the next little while. But it's really the truth.

Of course it doesn't feel good when someone rejects us or ditches us or treats us with very little respect or concern. Especially if there's a history of kindness and shared memories, of times when you really went out of your way to show up or to help. But if you are suddenly discarded, you'll probably look back and realize you were dealing with a mostly one-way street. Someone who genuinely cares about you will not treat you carelessly, no matter how caught up he or she might be with other interests.

And if someone is behaving in a disappointing way, that's no reflection on you, it's a reflection of where that person happens to be on her or his own path. You don't have to take it to heart. That doesn't mean it doesn't sting or hurt, it just means you don't have to take it as a sign that you're easy to discard. There's that great Eleanor Roosevelt quote, "You wouldn't worry so much about what others think of you if you realized how seldom they do."

Generally, you're dealing with one of two things: either you have some part in the dissolution of what was once a beautiful bond, but the other party is unwilling or unable to communicate in a respectful way so you can understand a differing point of view, and apologize if the situation warrants that, or, you're dealing with a person who truly doesn't give a sh%ot. And either way, it takes two to make a "thing go right." There's another song for you, you're welcome.

If a person won't tell you what's up, don't lose sleep over it. I mean, in order to own your end of a thing, a person has to be willing to tell you what the thing is, and if they won't, it really has to go in your, "no time for this" folder. Because that's okay in high school, but otherwise, not so much. And if a person doesn't care, why waste your precious time and energy on it?

The thing is, life is so short. All you can do is manage the way you show up, and pay attention to what you do. If you blow it, own it, apologize, and take some time for self-inquiry so you can learn and grow and do it better the next time. Try not to hurt people. If you're the person doing the leaving, whether we're talking about the end of a friendship or a romantic relationship, communication is always a good way to go. If you went on one date with someone and it wasn't a match, I'm not saying you have to spend an hour talking about why that is. But don't say you'll call if you have no intention of calling, because that's also only okay in high school, and not really even then. And if someone is into you and it isn't mutual, don't leave them hanging in the wind. People are precious and the human heart is tender. Take care of your own, and be kind to others. Simple, right?

Compassion for Those with No Compassion

How do you have compassion for people who seem incapable of having any for you? How do you practice patience with people who are full of venom and rage? First of all, you have to make yourself safe. If this is a person who has to be in your life, like a family member you're unwilling or unable to cut off, then boundaries are your priority. Once you've made yourself safe, then it's a matter of figuring out how to communicate in a way that feels okay to you. That might mean email only, or it might mean that you never leave yourself vulnerable. For example, if you grew up with an abusive parent, maybe it means you stay at a hotel when you go home to visit (assuming you want to visit at all). You don't put yourself in a vulnerable and powerless position. You protect your tender heart, and you put a high value on your own well-being, physically, mentally and emotionally.

I get a lot of emails from people who've been through an acrimonious divorce, and are unable to communicate with their exes in a healthy way. If you have children with someone, that's such a heartbreak for everyone involved, but sometimes there's no way around it. There are personality disorders that cause people to be incapable of understanding how things are for anyone but themselves. There are people who cling to their rage because it's the only shield they've got. There are people who truly revise history so it resembles something they can live with, where they get to be this wonderful person, and you get to be the villain. Again and again I'll remind you, you cannot save anyone. You're not going to "show someone the light" with your logic or your pleading or your version of history. Sometimes you're dealing with narcissism or borderline personality disorder, bipolar disorder or depression, sometimes you're dealing with addiction. In any of those cases, trying to reason isn't going to get you far.

The way to find compassion if you're dealing with

someone like this, is to understand they are in pain. Underneath all that rage and venom and instability, is a giant well of pain and anguish. And a lot of the time, people who are suffering this way truly believe their version of reality. There's nothing you can do except hope they're going to find relief at some point, and keep yourself at a safe distance in the meantime. Obviously you try to find help and support for people, but a person has to be ready to accept it, and then they have to be willing to work. That isn't always the case. And let me just say that having compassion for someone does not mean you allow them to harm you, or you excuse their cruel or abusive behavior. It means you recognize the pain, you understand you cannot fix it for them, and you find a way to deal with them while you also honor your own tender heart.

A lot of the time, we try to make things black and white, but they rarely are. So much of life and human behavior exists in the grey area. We like to make people "good" or "bad", but very few people are all one or the other. And sometimes we take things personally that have nothing to do with us. Sometimes you just represent something to someone. You're a convenient target because you seem happy or together or responsible or inspiring, and this other person feels none of those things. There's no need to engage or defend yourself when a person creates a fictional character and says that's who you are. If you know who you are, and you feel comfortable with the way you've handled yourself, or maybe you've apologized for your end, there's nothing more you need to do, except release yourself from the drama. Life is really too short for that. You can feel badly that someone is so stuck they have no recourse but to lash out, but you really don't have the time to participate in unraveling the fiction. It'll burn out eventually, anyway. There will be a new target, a new injustice.

As for strangers who do or say things you find totally incomprehensible, I'd say the same holds true. When people do things that are cruel or inhumane, you can bet they're coming out of a very unhappy environment. Maybe they were abused, neglected, abandoned. There are so many stories out there that just break your heart. When I see someone doing something or saying something I find repugnant, I also remind myself that that cannot be a happy way to move through life, filled with rage. And I wonder what happened to that person as a child, what went wrong along the way. I wonder how he or she learned to hate, or learned to close down or lash out. And on my good days, I try to send some love. That's all we can do, really.

CHAPTER 10: THE PATH TO LOVE AND HAPPINESS

In order to be at peace, it's essential that we know ourselves well and deeply, and that we learn to quiet the mind so we can be present. If you don't know what inspires you, or you haven't yet figured out what you're here to do, that's your first order of business. You have to know what brings you joy in order to know which way to move. If there are issues and wounds blocking your ability to tap into that well of wisdom within you, you have to get busy digging, and you might need some help with that.

If your mind is loud and full of should, there's no way to experience the beauty in life. Feelings of love, joy and gratitude happen in the now, they don't occur in the past or future. It's easy to get caught up in our lists of what isn't going right, and completely lose sight of all the gifts in our lives, but that perpetuates a cycle of longing and shame.

Opening to happiness often involves a mind-shift, a change in the way we're thinking about ourselves, other people, and the world at large. So much of the time, it's our own thinking that's making us sick and miserable. Culturally, we're taught to focus on the externals, as if something outside ourselves could solve the problem, but if you aren't happy, that's always inside work.

Love is the Best Answer You're Going to Get

If it were possible to have irrefutable answers to life's big questions, I'm pretty sure we'd have them by now. We arrive in this world, and we're received with love, or we aren't. We don't have to worry about a roof over our heads, or we do. We're afforded an excellent education, or we aren't. We have a stable home life, or we live in a war zone. We grow up being told what to think, or we're allowed to make our own way. The possibilities are endless, but we do have some things in common.

We deal with the same parameters, that's one thing. We're on this pale blue dot of a planet, and we don't know how long we get to be here, or how long our loved ones get to be here, either. We don't know for sure what happens after this. No one tells us the best use of our time and energy, or maybe lots of people do, but we all have to make sense of that on our own. We will all suffer to some degree or another, because this life, even if you have all the advantages in the world, is not an easy gig. It's wildly interesting, and there's always the potential for deep love, but along with that comes the potential for knifing loss, and that is not easy to face. We are inherently vulnerable. Some of us will experience the kind of loss that makes us question the point of it all.

But we have this incredible capacity to love, and a great desire to heal our old wounds. We might not have a lot of the answers, but most people who've been on the planet for awhile seem to agree that love and connection are the best experiences available to us. I mean, you know you have now. So what are you doing with your now? The greatest shortcut to happiness is to do whatever you can to uplift those around you. Giving feels good. Being seen and understood, cherished and celebrated not in spite of, but because of, all our flaws and all our beauty is a great gift. And it's beautiful to give that to other people, too. Listening deeply, caring with your whole being, these things feel amazing. And they're available, every day. You can get caught up in your plans and ideas, you can join in the race, but I really think the better focus is the moments. How can you love with your whole heart, today?

If you're brave enough to get quiet, to sit up tall for a few minutes, and to feel yourself breathing in and breathing out, you will feel a connection to everyone and everything. That simple act will bring you right into the now, and now is where you need to be if you want to feel love, joy, gratitude and peace. You can't be in yesterday or tomorrow, you have to be in this moment. Being present feels good. You don't need to buy anything in order to experience that calm, that steadiness. If you want answers, they don't reside in a place or in another person. The answers you need are always inside. And those are the only answers you're going to get. Ultimately, you have to make sense out of this world yourself. If you take the time to create peace within you, you'll experience it around you, and you'll be spreading it wherever you go. We have tremendous power to affect the way our lives feel. Of course there are devastating things that can happen to any of us. But it's how we face what we're given.

We experience our life as if it has a beginning, middle and end. We treat this like it's our personal story, but that isn't it. We're joining a much larger story. We're in the flow, and then we're out of it. The flow goes on without us, although what we contribute while we're here certainly affects it, and those ripples continue on. But it's not your story, or mine. There are currently about seven billion of us contributing to this dance. What kind of dance are you doing while you're here?

Being present means we're opening to things as they are and trying to come back with love. We can focus on everything we don't have, or we can direct our attention to those gifts we do have. Part of quieting the storm that rages in the mind involves choosing the thoughts that will strengthen us. Yes, there are things that can make us sick from the outside, but a lot of the time it's our own thinking that's causing us to suffer. We can argue about all kinds of things, but it's pointless. We're all in this mystery together. We can get caught up in names, borders, colors, religions and opinions. But love is the best answer you're going to get.

Let Love Do That

A big part of being at peace involves our ability to sit with discomfort. Not everything in life feels good, or is easy to deal with or comprehend. Sometimes we are the source of our greatest discomfort, and sometimes other people or the events around us give us an opportunity to lean into our fear, our rage, our guilt, grief or shame. It isn't easy, but it's how we learn and grow.

We all have our stuff, and even if you do the work to heal, to become intimately acquainted with the source of your pain, the things that trigger you, or the thoughts and tendencies that weaken you, it's likely that you'll have to grapple with them from time to time, because you're hu-

153

man and this is no easy gig. But a lot of the time, we resist and contract against our own experience, especially if it's messy, complicated, disappointing or uncomfortable. Maybe we've made a mess—said something or done something we wish we hadn't in a moment of weakness or anger or confusion, or maybe we've been on the receiving end of poor treatment. Perhaps it's circumstances that have us pushed to our edge; mostly, life does not unfold according to the vision we had in our heads of "how things should be."

The source of addiction is this feeling that we can't take it. We can't withstand this temporary feeling, we have to do something, now. The best thing to do is have a seat and breathe. Because if you drink the feeling away, or pop a pill, or go shopping or hop in the sack with someone, that feeling will just arise again in the not too distant future. It won't go away unless you face it down. Unless you examine the root of your discomfort, it will direct your life. And no feeling is forever. If you practice leaning into your painful feelings, you'll find they arise, peak and subside like every other living thing.

The very best thing you can do when you feel "pushed up against it" is to breathe. Fighting reality will not change it. You don't have to put everything in the thank you column, you don't have to be grateful for every experience in your life. Some things are devastating and will never make sense, but you can always grow from your pain. You can use your suffering to become softer, more open, more empathetic. That's so much better than resisting, denying, numbing out or running. The longer you do that, the longer your pain owns you. And you know what? I wouldn't let pain own you, I'd let love do that.

It's Already Eight Minutes Ago

The other night I was watching "Cosmos" on Netflix with my kids. In this particular episode, Neil deGrasse Tyson was explaining how it takes eight minutes for the light of the sun to reach the earth. So when we look at the sun, we're really looking at the way the sun looked eight minutes ago. We never see it in real time. By the same token, when we look at a sunset, we're seeing the image of the way the sun set eight minutes ago; what we're watching has already happened.

The episode also covered astronomer William Herschel, and his son John, who, amongst many other contributions, advanced the science of photography as we know it today. He grew up hearing about the stars from his father, who also explained to young John that many of the stars in the sky were not really there any longer. If the sun we see is really the sun from eight minutes ago, and many of the stars we see are no longer there, it's all too understandable that we'd want to uncover what is real. And that the son of a man who spoke of such things would want to learn how to capture a moment in time.

Anyway, I'm sure I learned about the eight-minute time lapse at some point, but I guess it didn't stick in my mind the way it did this time. I looked at the sun a lot today, and kept thinking, "I'm looking at the past." I mean, if we look up and the sun we're seeing is the sun of eight minutes ago, how can any of us think we have a second to waste? Everything in the universe is in a constant state of motion. The earth, the sun, the stars, the galaxies, our feelings, relationships, and us, ourselves—we come and we go.

And it made me think about Instagram and our obsession with documenting everything. Some people are a little more obsessed than others, but it seems we're all trying to say, "Look! I'm here, right?" And, "Here I am!" You go to watch your kid playing soccer or baseball, or you go to the Glee Club concert, and you wonder, "What must the kids think?" They look in the stands, or out into the audience, and they can't make eye contact with their parents. They can't even see mom's or dad's faces, all they can see are phones.

Of course it's fine to document things from time to time. Most people enjoy looking at pictures from their childhood, or the meaningful moments in their lives as they grew into adults. But now, it's like we're documenting everything, all the time. "Look at this juice I just drank! I'm here! I exist!" And the thing is, the second you're talking about what you're doing, the second you're thinking about it, you aren't in it anymore. You've taken yourself outside the experience.

There's a reason people (not all people, but let's say a decent majority), love sex. You lose yourself. At least, you do if the sex is great and there's a lot of feeling between you and your partner. You aren't taking yourself out of the experience to document how you feel about it. "Hmmm, I'm enjoying this. This is great. Let me try to catch it from this angle so I can tweet about it." Well, maybe some people are, but if we're talking about truly great sex we are completely in and of the moment. Sex is not the only place we can experience this, obviously.

You can get lost in nature on an incredible hike. You can unroll your yoga mat and get lost in the breath and other sensations in the body. You can get lost in a great book, you can become immersed in creating a delicious meal, you can salsa dance your way into losing yourself.

The thing is, it's vital that you find a way to do just that, and frequently. Because when you lose that small self, that self full of ideas about who you are and who other people are and what you need and what you should have and how life should look and what that other person said or did and why that movie actually really sucked even though it won an Oscar and everyone else seems to be seeing something you aren't, and Oh.My.God. When you can actually shut all that down and just join the flow and be present, you can also experience your true self. Your open, curious, engaged, immersed self. Your should-less self. And that is so important to do, because when you do that you. YOU. You are present. You are present enough to recognize that the earth is spinning and some of the stars are already gone, already gone and the sun is shining the way it did eight minutes ago and you. You are part of all of that. You're made of the same stuff as that sun and those stars and you are also spinning and moving and changing, and one day there will be a glimmer of you, a spark of you, a mark left by you, because you are here and you do matter, even if every moment of your life is not documented you are here. Don't miss it. Don't miss it.

Rest in Your True Nature

Yoga is a process of coming home to yourself. It's a science, an art, a philosophy of stripping away anything that isn't part of your authentic self. So much of the time, we've gotten confused along the way. We've taken on other people's beliefs or ideas or philosophies and accepted them as our own, without question. Hatred can be taught this way, so can compassion. If you were lucky, your first influences taught you that you were of value. That you had an impact on the world around you. That it mattered how you felt. If you were fortunate, you were also taught that being kind and thinking about how your actions affect other people and the world around you would help you to connect and thrive.

Sometimes we have a lot of unlearning to do, though. Maybe we were not so lucky, and we learned that only certain feelings were okay, and that we had to repress anything that made the people around us feel uncomfortable or inadequate, like our sadness or our anger or our loneliness. There are so many people who reach adulthood and have no clue how they really feel, because they cut themselves off from their own intuition years ago.

If you come out of an abusive background you can count on having to unlearn quite a lot. Growing up in an environment where you make yourself invisible or invaluable depending on the moment requires a total suppression of anything that has to do with what you really need or want in your heart.

So many people are on the run, owned by their painful feelings. Repressed rage turns into depression. It takes a Herculean effort to push down an active volcano. So much energy, in fact, there isn't much left to do anything else. Thus the lethargy and hopelessness.

For some people, it's easy to say yes when yes is in their hearts, and it's not difficult to say no when the situation warrants. But other people have to work to figure out what a yes feels like. And those same people might have to learn to give themselves permission to say no. Feeling that your worth is determined by other people's perceptions of you sets you up for a lifetime of powerlessness.

Anyway, my point is, there are so many differing ways people might need to come home to themselves. And all of the ways that work require determination and dedication. You have to find the discipline to show up for yourself, and to lean in when you'd rather take off. If you find that what you've been doing isn't working, and by that I mean, if life is not feeling good to you, it's time to try something new, because time waits for none of us.

There are eight "limbs" in yoga practice. The physical part, the "asana" is just one limb. It's a very useful entry point for many of us in the west, because we value doing over being, and it takes time to undo that programming. When you connect to your breath (pranayama), you also connect to something that is happening right now, in this moment. You are present and aware. When you start to organize your body into a pose, when you focus on lengthening your spine, or relaxing your shoulders, you're also giving the mind a focal point that's happening in the now. So you use your body to quiet your mind. If you're paying attention to your breath, or you feel your feet on the floor, you aren't spinning anymore. You aren't fretting over your past or freaking out about your future, you are present, and that's beautiful because life isn't happening in your rear-view mirror or somewhere out in front of you. When you create space between your thoughts, you also create space to connect to that most authentic part of yourself. You get to breathe in that space.

Your body is full of wisdom about who you are and what you need to be at peace. It knows where you're holding on, resisting, or contracting from your experience. If you give it the chance and you set up a compassionate and kind inner environment, your body will give these things over, it will help you to let go of those ideas or beliefs that are weighing you down. And then you can fly.

Get Sweaty

I think many people out there are miserable because

their expectations are unrealistic. If, for example, you're thinking you're going to reach some point in your evolution when you're ecstatic every moment of every day, I think you're going to be disappointed, and I don't believe you're ever going to reach that place. It seems many people are searching for the "high highs", and as a result, they find themselves dealing with the "low lows." The thing is, happiness is not a destination, it's born from your process.

When we get caught up in the externals, in the results, in the material proof of our successes, we're way off the path of what brings us true fulfillment and satisfaction. An object will never be able to provide you with feelings of worth or meaning for long. Neither will an altered state of consciousness. Nor will another human being. What do you spend most of your time doing? Really look at that. Because most of your time adds up to most of your life, and if you're spending a large majority of it feeling dissatisfied, or like you're just punching a clock, or doing what you're "supposed" to be doing, I wouldn't expect life to feel very good for you, regardless of your bank account. In other words, you might be making lots of money and accruing lots of stuff, but if you don't love the way you're spending your days, it won't amount to a happy life.

And happy doesn't mean perfect. I know we see all of our friends with their shiny Instagram lives and pithy status updates, but please understand everyone goes through the same stuff. The people who are genuinely happy with their lives still have their struggles, their challenges, their days when they don't feel like getting out of their pajamas. It's not "all good", and it's not all positive, and you don't have to be grateful for every experience you've ever been through, or every loss you've yet to endure. It's a tough gig, being human. It's awesome, it's wonderful, it's interesting, but it's not easy. And we get sold a false bill of goods, and sent down an unfulfilling path until we wise up and get right with ourselves.

Take a look at what you're contributing, and how you feel about it. Working toward something you believe in feels great, but it's not easy. Take a look at the people with whom you're spending your time. It's one of your most precious gifts; that, and your energy. And sometimes when we step back from the "grind", or the "rat-race", we realize we're giving our time and energy to pursuits and people who weaken us, rather than strengthen us. And maybe we remember it shouldn't be a grind, and we aren't rats. Obviously there are the practicalities of life. We have to be able to feed and clothe ourselves, we have to keep a roof over our heads, and if we're responsible for other people, we have to make sure they're taken care of as well. But what lights you up? What feeds your soul? What excites you, scares you, inspires you? These are questions you'll have to answer if you want to be at peace.

That's my definition of what it means to be happy. It means you're feeling good about the way you're living your life. It means you've figured out what your particular gifts are, and you've found a way to share them. Does that way have to be the thing that keeps a roof over your head? No, not necessarily. I think that's ideal, but I think the main thing is to be sure you're devoting a nice chunk of your time to those pursuits that bring you joy, and that offer you an opportunity to share what's in your heart.

Self-acceptance is another huge part of the puzzle. If you despise yourself, you're not going to be happy. Obvious, yes? If you have healing to do, there's simply no avoiding it. If you're enraged, or in a cycle of blame and shame, you're going to have to move right into the center of your pain and have a seat. You do not have to stay there for the rest of your life, so don't tell yourself it's too hard. What's too hard is living your whole life feeling frustrated and lost. Sitting with, examining, and understanding your issues, your pitfalls, your raw places and those tendencies that aren't serving you, are the very things you need to do to liberate yourself from a lifetime of suffering. You can't avoid your rage, or internalize it, or attach it to people outside yourself, or numb it out and think it's going to go away, because it won't. You have to deal with the source, and that's deeply uncomfortable, painful work, but it's also finite. Once you have a thorough understanding of why you feel the way you do and have, it will lose its grip on you.

This is the way it works. I'm not saying you'll never have to deal with it again, I'm just saying this stuff will not own you anymore, it won't rule your life, your behavior, and your choices. It won't show up in its unrelenting way and block you from feeling a sustained sense of meaning, purpose and peace. Then you can go about the business of figuring out how you want to spend your time, and with whom, and how you're going to share your gifts. And if you start to do your days like that, you'll find you're having some pretty happy and fulfilling weeks, months, years and decades. It's not what we have, it's what we give. Focus on giving, and the having takes care of itself. You'll always have enough with this formula, because what you'll have is meaning and purpose.

Lastly, take this literally several times a week: get sweaty. Feel your heart pumping. Remember you have a body, and use it and move it. Become your breath and your heartbeat and your sensations, and get out of your loud mind with its relentless and obsessive thoughts. Yoga is great for that; that is actually the purpose of yoga–to calm the storm that rages in the mind. It's not about turning yourself into a pretzel, it's a way of moving through life. It's about the quality you're bringing to whatever it is you're doing. We practice being present on our mats, so we can be present in our lives.

Tackle It

Sometimes people get really clear on what their tendencies are, but that's as far as they go. Maybe you know people like this. I used to date a guy who was brilliant in this regard. If something came up between us and I talked to him about how I felt, he would focus and listen and completely own his end. He could tell me what had driven him to do what he did, or say what he'd said. He would acknowledge that he understood why I would feel the way I did, and he'd apologize. And I'd think, awesome. He really heard me. We understand each other. We've had some really good communication. But then the next time a similar situation presented itself, nothing at all would change.

Identifying our stuff is a huge step. It's definitely a big part of knowing ourselves, so we can be accountable for the energy we're spreading and the actions we're taking. But if that's as far as we go, we've landed in a ditch. Sometimes I get emails from people, and they say things like, "Well, I have an addictive personality, so sometimes I lie." And I'll ask, "Is that the end of the story? You have an addictive personality, so you lie?" Or I'll hear, "My dad left when I was four, so I have abandonment issues." I may have said that once or twice in my life. The thing is, your abandonment issues don't make it okay for you to cling or manipulate or bend over backwards to be perfect so people won't leave you. Life isn't going to feel good like that. And this is my point. Knowing what your issues are is huge. Then you can be aware when you're in a danger zone. If you have fear of being left and you keep picking people who are unavailable, you can rightly assume you still have some healing to do around the first time you felt abandoned. You don't have to let that one ancient event predetermine your whole destiny. You don't have to keep replaying the old tape again and again.

Other classic examples of identification without the follow-up work? "I have fear of commitment", "I have fear of failure", "I felt invisible as a kid so I need attention all the time", "I felt invisible as a kid, so I cringe when people notice me", "I learned you can't trust anyone, so I don't." You get the picture. It's what we do about what we know that matters. If you have fear of being abandoned, that's yours to grapple with and tame. It's not your partner's work, it's yours. Do you want to choose people who are compassionate when you're going to be intimate? Of course. Do you want to be able to share your struggles and allow yourself to be vulnerable? Yes. But your pain and disappointments and heartbreaks do not give you free rein to act out all over the place. It's never okay to check your partner's emails or text messages, even if your last partner cheated on you, or you grew up in a house where infidelity was the norm. That has nothing to do with your partner, and it is not their job to allow you to violate their privacy because you feel triggered. Having a conversation about your feelings is fine. But even that will get old after awhile. A therapist is a great call if you're struggling with internal demons.

I can tell you I slayed quite a few on my yoga mat, and in a therapist's office. I find that to be a winning combination. Therapy is a great place to become aware of what's scaring you, or blocking you from living life in a way that feels good to you. And a yoga mat is a great place to start to starve the voice that tells you this is how you are, or this is how things are. You don't have to believe everything you think, as the saying goes. Everyone is different, of course. And part of the work is searching for healing modalities and combinations that are going to work for you.

In order to liberate ourselves from our issues, we have to heal the original wounds we're carrying. We can't play this stuff out in the present and expect that to be the balm that soothes us, because in order to create a similar dynamic of pain, you'll have to pick people who cannot give you what you want. That's the hook. That's what snags you. All you'll accomplish that way is the creation of more pain for yourself, and more information that affirms your false thesis statement that "everyone leaves", or "everyone cheats", or whatever it is you're telling yourself. If you want to heal, you'll have to dive into the source of your pain and face it head on. This is the only way I know to free yourself. If you could run, I'd tell you to run. If you could solve it by pretending it isn't there, I'd say go ahead, pretend. If you could numb it without killing yourself in the process, I'd say do your thing. And if you could heal by replaying ancient pain in your present, with people who don't know how to do anything but hurt you, I'd say have at it. But none of that works. You're just on a train, crashing into a wall. And that becomes less and less pleasant, no matter how many words and explanations you give it. Who cares why you're crashing into a brick wall? At a certain point, don't you want to just not do that anymore?

It's wonderful to be able to know yourself and articulate how things are for you. But ultimately, these things are more interesting to us than they will be to anyone else. And they're more useful to us, as well. Stopping at the identification process is like picking a dish off the menu, but not eating it. Time to grab your fork if you need to!

Don't Miss the View

There are two ways to do life. One way seems like the easy way. You follow the status quo and decide it's all about what you have and how you look and who you're with, and you devote all your time and energy to these things and find ways to numb yourself out from the absurdity of it all. You do this with food or drugs or sex or stuff, but most of the time you feel miserable and tired. You think things like, "What's the point of it all?"

The other way seems like the hard way. You face your fears. You listen to that small but truthful voice inside you that says, "There is NO WAY this life is about how big your butt is, or your bank account, can we please get real? There's a life to live here that is beautiful and amazing, there's a song you need to be singing, what, exactly, are you doing???" And you get busy.

You get busy paying attention, listening deeply, acknowledging your pain, doing the work. You stop chasing happiness in the form of "stuff", and you start chasing the truth (I mean what is true for you). You probably feel sick to your stomach and lonely and scared and like you must be crazy for walking away from your comfort zone and all the people waving you back like the Wild Things. But comfort zones are located in the middle. You cannot see the incredible view from there.

That may seem like the hard way, and it is brutal for awhile, there's no doubt. Getting real is a painful process of shedding anything you've taken on that isn't authentic to you, including ways of thinking and being. It hurts. But it is so much better to move through your pain for awhile, realize what you know, remember who you are, discover why you're here, and take your gorgeous self right out to the edge of life, where the sun is stunningly bright and yellow and orange and pink and you can be your true self. You can stand with your feet on the ground and your heart wide open, and just be awed by all the beauty and suffering, all the love and confusion, all the light and darkness. And you can sing the song of compassion and add your colors to this incredible life, this chaotic, mysterious, mind-bending experience. When it breaks your heart wide open, you can cry a real, true cry, right from your gut. And when it amazes you, you can receive the gifts with gratitude and love and delight. We have this thing backwards. The easy way is the hard way. The hard way is only hard for awhile. Then it's awesome. Pick awesome. Start walking. Awesome won't wait, and you do not want to miss it.

You Can't Offer the Shirt Off Your Back if You're Naked

You cannot trust yourself until you heal yourself. It's a sad fact, but if you've avoided your own pain through denial or numbing or running or repressing, you've only succeeded in feeding it power. And as long as you're suffering, your pain will spill out on those who come close to you. You know whether you're "right with yourself" or you aren't; it's no secret to you. You are aware if you've done the work to heal or you haven't, and you also know whether love is at your center. (It is, but it may be buried under rage or blame or resentment, and if you haven't walked through that fire, you're just burning in it).

Maya Angelou speaks about this, "I do not trust people who don't love themselves and yet tell me, 'I love you.' There is an African saying which is: Be careful when a naked person offers you a shirt." If you want to trust yourself, you have to find the courage to stop numbing your pain, and instead invite it, embrace it, and hold it up to the light. Otherwise anything you've pushed down owns you, your choices, and your behavior. You have to be willing to let your heart break open, and to be brave enough to be soft. That's the only way to heal yourself, and it's also the only way to trust yourself. Because you won't heal without truly understanding who you are, without releasing the heat of painful events you may have been carrying with you for years, without understanding your blind spots, your tendencies and your outlook. You won't heal until you know yourself deeply, and until you accept all parts of who you are, even those things that are hard to acknowledge.

Once you see yourself clearly and kindly, once you love yourself and understand what a gift you are, even with your flaws and your scars and your fears and your pain, then you can do that for other people, too, you can love with your heart wide open. If you're coming from love, believe me, you can trust yourself. You can feel assured that your actions and responses will be coming from a strong center. You'll still make plenty of mistakes, but they won't be motivated by places within you that haven't been explored, that are cloaked in darkness.

Love gives us the strength to sit with painful feelings without acting on them. Love is not going to sing "Kumbaya" all the time, or tell you or anyone else that "it's all good." It isn't all good. Sometimes people will say things and do things that are careless or thoughtless or hurtful or cruel, manipulative or aggressive or dishonest. Sometimes you will, too. Love is like a mirror; you cannot lie to it, it's just going to reflect back whatever the truth may be. There's no hiding in love, it's a naked, vulnerable experience, and sometimes love is gonna let you know you blew it and have some work to do.

What's beautiful is that when love says "no", you can believe it. You can trust it. And when you trust yourself, you will know how to live. You will recognize the no's and embrace the yeses, you will know what you need to feed your soul and keep growing and opening and challenging yourself to love more and heal more and give more, and also when to rest. Knowing how to live so that you can honor yourself and still face reality as it is, is a gift to you and everyone you encounter, and a true liberation. Wishing that for you, and sending love, as always,

Ally Hamilton

ACKNOWLEDGEMENTS

It might seem strange from the outside, but I want to start by thanking my ex-husband, and still-business partner, Dorian Cheah. We've been on a wild ride the last six years with the creation of our third, and most challenging child, Yogis Anonymous. It has been exhilarating and frustrating and exhausting, and very, very fulfilling to try to spread this incredible practice across the globe. This book would not exist if he hadn't encouraged me to share on the Facebook page the way he did. There would be no blog, and no forthcoming book, either. There would be no site and no recording of classes. And of course, more than anything else, there would be no Dylan or Devyn. Thank you for everything you bring to my life, and to the studio and the site, which is often behind-the-scenes, but essential to everything. And thank you for being a great Daddy.

Next, I have to again thank and acknowledge my wonderful agent, Dana Newman, who has become a true friend. So thankful to have such a wise, funny, talented woman to have my back. I also want to thank in advance Angela Wix at Llewellyn Worldwide, my wonderful editor on the forthcoming book, "Yoga's Healing Power: Looking Inward for Change, Growth and Peace" for all of her insight, suggestions, and willingness to talk things out.

I have to thank my first reader of both books, longtime student and friend, Elizabeth Quayle for her enthusiasm and encouragement. Dani Shapiro, Mark Sarvas, and Claire Bidwell Smith offered support, invaluable insight, some hand-holding and a lot of laughs throughout the creation of both books, and I don't know what I would have done without them. Josh Nelson, Anne Lilburn, Bob DeMaa, Adam Smith, and Alex Karlin have been taking class for years and are my second family. Jessica Perez Bricke (who created the wonderful cover for this book, and the lotus flower/fortune cookie I had in my head) is always there to lend an ear or a shoulder, a hug or a laugh. So grateful to have each of you in my life.

Wendy Greenberg Doucette and Tracy Bleier are more sisters than friends. I've shared more laughs and tears with these women than anyone else, and it has been a true gift in my life to travel with such amazing, funny, loving, thoughtful and inspiring women.

I want to thank my boyfriend, Dr. Jay Pietrzak, for all the love, support, respect and laughter along the way, and for scrambling my eggs into the shape of a heart every morning. Thank you for never taking the days or the moments for granted, I'm so lucky to have you in my life.

I want to thank my family, my mom and stepdad, my little brother, and my father. Thank you for being each of you, and for allowing me to write about you. I hope I do a good enough job as a parent that I won't be bothered if my kids decide to write about me one day. I love each of you from the bottom of my heart, and am glad and grateful for everything.

And to Dylan and Devyn. Thank you for teaching me everything I need to know about love. Thank you for amazing me every day. Thank you for showing up in my life, and being exactly who you are. There aren't words for the gratitude I have for you, but hopefully I show you every single day. I love you both to the moon and back, and all around the universe, Mommy.

27962167R00115

Made in the USA
Middletown, DE
27 December 2015